RESCUING YOUR LOCAL ECONOMY
Success Stories for Sustainable Communities

FRANCIS P. KOSTER, ED.D.

www.theoptimisticfuturist.org
futuristfran@aol.com

ISBN 13: 978-1530496471
ISBN 10: 1530496470

Cover Design: Walter Stanford
www.WalterStanford.com

Book Design: Kenneth Guentert
The Publishing Pro, LLC
Colorado Springs, Colorado

B16-3

This book is dedicated to Fred and Alice Stanback, in recognition of their tireless and generous advocacy for improved public policy.

TABLE OF CONTENTS

To my wife, Carol Spalding, Ed.D., without whose patience, loving support, and critical pen this work would not have survived.

And to all of my talented children (Caila, Josh, Alex, and Raph) and their significant others, each of whom brings overlapping gifts of intelligence, creativity, and loving suggestions for improvement whenever I request them—and occasionally when I didn't, but should have. I love you all.

Also making significant contributions were Giles Hopkins, Jean Kadela, and Janice Silver for skillful editing and error checking. Their unique gifts were of inestimable value.

None of the work would be in your hands without the patience, guidance, and wisdom of Kenneth Guentert, whose company identity, The Publishing Pro, is both a fair company name and a good description of the man.

Cover illustration by
Walter Stanford
www.WalterStanford.com

Introduction

If you are reading this introduction, it is likely that we share an emotional connection—we have both experienced or witnessed first hand the pain and loss caused by a failing local economy and we want to do something to rescue our own communities.

We both have seen how a failing local economy causes sickness, increases divorce, increases crime, results in stressed schools, and how it fractures the social networks that could otherwise create that powerful sense of place where we each feel we belong.

Perhaps, like me, you have witnessed friends whose lives were devastated by the impact of a failing local economy: job loss, illness, and even loss of children. Or perhaps we both have seen communities badly harmed by environmental contamination.

Perhaps like me, you have also felt overwhelmed by the complexity and persistence of these challenges, but refuse to give up. This book is for you. The stories in this book will provide you with both the inspiration and the practical guidance for how you can make an impact in your own community.

You will learn how communities are:

- Increasing the life expectancy of the poor while creating jobs
- Improving the health of newborns by reducing the exposure of expectant mothers to environmental toxins and lowering public health-care costs
- Growing the food production sector of your local economy while successfully fighting the obesity epidemic
- Increasing local renewable energy production, while creating local employment
- Improving schools by successfully addressing the ever increasing percentage of young students with learning difficulties while making your community attractive to young families
- Reducing the number of repeat offenders filling our jails by helping them create small business opportunities that break the cycle of incarceration

There are common themes in the success stories that make these solutions sustainable:

- Fostering the growth and opportunities that can come from the unique form of capitalism in the U.S.

- Making investments that are proven to reduce the number of people or companies that need or are given taxpayer support
- Expanding the production of local goods and services
- Converting waste products to generate income or reduce expenses
- Creating systems to help citizens meet their basic needs through alternatives to the cash economy
- Building a healthy living environment

In many cases, the secret to the sustained success of these efforts was an insight that enabled the community leadership to recognize assets they did not know they had.

Don't put the book down. Pick a community problem you have the passion to solve and read about the secrets to success that other communities have discovered. Then mobilize your friends and neighbors and use these examples to create success in your own community.

Creating A Sustainable Local Economy

A failing local economy causes sickness, both mental and physical.

On the other hand, so can an "improving" economy — if it is not guided to be sustainable.

One of the reasons that this pain is not part of economic discussions is that the terms used to discuss the health of the economy are badly flawed. A society can have a rise in the following three commonly used measures of economic success, while actually declining in prosperity.

The three widely used terms that mislead:

1) Gross Domestic Product (GDP) measures money earned and circulated — so if a child gets hurt and requires surgery, GDP goes up, because the doctor makes more money and the child loses no wages. But if the doctor gets hurt, GDP goes down because she does not earn while recovering. Not a useful measurement when trying to improve society.

2) The "Unemployment Rate." As commonly used, it does not count the unemployed. It only counts a narrow slice of them, because if the jobless worker goes back to school, they are not counted. If they lose a high paying job and take a much lower paying job, they are "employed." If they stop reporting to a state agency that they are looking

for work they are not counted. If they stop looking for work after months and months of searching because there are no jobs out there, they are not counted.

If you flip the metric around, and count the "employed," you don't get closer to the truth about the quality of life in society either. It is possible to have a rising employment rate while lowering the standard of living for the entire country.

One example: for every twelve jobs in the sector of the U.S. economy that mines, transports, or burns coal to make electricity, one innocent American dies each year from the health effects of burning it, and many more get serious illnesses.[1] Counting increased employment without looking at collateral damage created by it is misleading. There are many similar examples.

3) Average life expectancy. Consider this: in 2015, compared to prior years, life expectancy for a poor American

---

1   According to the Bureau of Labor Statistics, there are 91,600 employees working in coal mining in the United States, 46,000 more transport the coal to the utility, and 21,000 burn it to make electricity, for a total of 158,600 jobs. In 2010, statisticians analyzed EPA data about the impact of coal-fired electricity on the health of the general population. They found the smoggy air pollution from coal-fired electric generation kills 13,200 Americans annually. Divide 158,600 by 13,200, and you get one dead for each twelve jobs. Additionally, the same data showed that burning coal annually causes 20,000 heart attacks, 12,000 hospital admissions, and costs our society over $100 billion per year in health-care expenses. Divide 158,600 jobs into $100 billion in annual coal-caused health-care costs and you get an annual public health cost of $630,000 per coal-industry job per year.

woman fell in 43 percent of American counties. During the same time period, national "average life expectancy" is shown to be rising, because the other 57 percent of the counties showed increases in years lived. The increases in the lucky counties were greater than the decline in the unlucky counties, so the "average life expectancy" went up. When a seesaw carries one child high and the other low, measuring the height of the middle is not always helpful. The use of the word "average" in economic discussions has the potential to conceal as much as it discloses.

To sum up: We have a rising rate of pain and suffering in segments of our society, masked by misleading vocabulary that celebrates one kind of economic impact and ignores others. All of the pain and suffering captured in these examples above shows we need to rethink the definition of "economic growth" to include the concept of sustainability. The good news is that others have already done it, in ways that every community in the U.S. can imitate. This section gives examples of that.

To Rebuild Failing Economies, Anticipate the Future

Each time Wal-Mart, Target, or Kmart opens a new store, fourteen smaller "mom and pop" stores die.[1] Between 1962 and 2013 these giants established more than 8,000 stores.[2] Most of these car-accessible big-box stores were located near interstate exits; most of the walkable smaller shops were located in the older downtown areas. Good-bye downtown.

While this was going on, one out of every two U.S. manufacturing jobs vanished[3]—either relocated overseas, displaced by automation, or both. This was a double whammy, because each highly paid local worker circulated enough money throughout the local economy to "trickle-down" another 4.6 local jobs.[4] When the manufacturing jobs vanished, so did many of the 4.6 local jobs. Good-bye downtown.

All across the United States, groups are meeting to plan the next steps for recreating downtowns. In many cases, they will be tripped up by something they are not expecting.

1   *Social Science Quarterly*, "Business Churn and the Retail Giant: Establishment Birth and Death from Wal-Mart's Entry," Carlena Cochi Ficano 24 Apr 2012

2   Ibid.

3   http://www.economicpopulist.org/content/offshoring-sea-shining-sea

4   http://www.uic.edu/cuppa/data/CUED_Manufacturing_Jobs_May2013.pdf

They cannot see these inevitable challenges because they envision their new design as though they were aiming a basketball toward a hoop that is, and will remain, stable. The fact is that their basketball must go through a hoop that is actually a moving target.

Around the planning table the word manufacturing will be used, and many people will have a mental picture of their dad on a factory shop floor holding a tool, rather than as an office worker programming a 3D printer. If the term food production comes up, the same people might imagine red barns and acres of green pastures, rather than indoor fish farms or hydroponic lettuce grown in old abandoned factories and delivered by electric cars.

To paraphrase Jack Welch, former CEO of General Electric, "If the world outside your organization is changing faster than your organization is changing, you lose."

The world outside is changing faster than any of us can imagine. The internet began to be widely used just twenty years ago. The first smartphone was introduced just over twenty years ago, and today the United States has more cell phones than citizens.[1] In the breadbasket region of the U.S., the worst drought in 1,000 years is already underway and beginning to disrupt food supplies.[2] The cost of beef has doubled since 2009.[3] Renewable energy prices (down 50 percent since 2010)[4] are predicted by Deutsche Bank

1   CTIA- The Wireless Association. www.ctia.org/growth

2   http://news.nationalgeographic.com/news/2015/02/150212-mega-drought-southwest-water-climate-environment/

3   http://www.nbcnews.com/business/economy/meat-prices-expected-keep-climbing-2015-n276906

4   http://cleantechnica.com/2012/03/14/ultra-thin-solar-cell-company-

to become competitive with all traditional energy sources (coal, oil and natural gas) by 2017,[1] resulting in much more locally built and locally maintained renewable energy.

Think of your downtown in 2035. The U.S. population will have grown by 20 percent.[2] The number of adults over 65 will be almost double what it is today,[3] and four in ten of those will need long-term care for two or more years.[4] The number of 85-year-olds will triple.[5] Since approximately one-third of all lifetime health-care costs are incurred during the last six months of life,[6] there will be a massive need for expanded health care for the elderly, and it will need to be located close to where they live.

Other changes already underway include household size, which in 1960 was three people living under one roof but now sits at two-and-a-half people. The average is expected to drop to about two people living in the same home.[7] We can also say with some certainty that twenty years from now we will see a great increase in interconnected electronic

unstealths-aims-to-cut-cost-of-solar-cells-in-half-images/

1   http://cleantechnica.com/2015/01/14/deutsche-bank-predicts-solar-grid-parity-80-global-market-2017/

2   http://www.statista.com/statistics/183481/united-states-population-projection/

3   https://www.census.gov/prod/2014pubs/p25-1141.pdf

4   http://www.rwjf.org/content/dam/farm/reports/issue_briefs/2014/rwjf410654

5   http://commons.wikimedia.org/wiki/File:USpop2010.svg

6   http://www.medicarenewsgroup.com/context/understanding-medicare-blog/understanding-medicare-blog/2013/06/03/end-of-life-care-constitutes-third-rail-of-u.s.-health-care-policy-debate

7   http://www.statista.com/statistics/183648/average-size-of-house-holds-in-the-us/

devices, individualized medicine instead of "one size fits all" pills, more medical care delivered at the pharmacy, education delivered to individual students electronically, and more neighbors who speak English as a second language. In addition, fewer people will own cars, instead using rent-by-the-hour cars picked up at some parking spot identified via a cell phone search. Industry is planning to introduce driverless cars. Many more people will work multiple part-time jobs from home. More people will commute by high-speed rail built along existing train lines.

Most of this change is already surfacing, but it has not yet been integrated into community planning for the future.

We can see that downtowns will need to have small elevator-equipped apartments with walkable access to life's basic needs, like grocery stores and pharmacies. Many of these apartments could be located above stores. All buildings (including those "spec" built to spur economic development) should be energy efficient and renewable-ready. Roofs should be designed to carry solar cells; electrical circuits should be constructed so that plugging in renewables is not a big chore once installed. Medical care will have to be close by, rather than near the large hospital miles away from those who are likely to need it most. Broadband should be everywhere—and affordable.

As you consider how to apply the tools for success you are about to be introduced to, remember that you are creating a society that has to meet a different set of needs than are visible today, which you can do by using fantastic new technology and ideas.

Underused Techniques Help Civil Servants and Chambers of Commerce Grow the Local Economy

Create Macrojobs
with Microlending

As I write this book, approximately 9 percent of workers in the United States are unemployed.[1] This does not tell the entire story, as only 4.2 percent of college graduates are unemployed, compared to 14 percent of those who did not finish high school.[2]

Simultaneously, banks and credit unions have limited lending to anyone except those with the highest credit ratings. And even entrepreneurs who have college educations and good credit ratings find it difficult to get a loan. Entrepreneurs who lack higher education and who suffer from a bruised credit history are finding it impossible. As a result our whole society loses, because without available capital, job development slows or stops completely.

Now consider this: small firms accounted for 65 percent of the net new jobs created between 1993 and 2009.[3] They represented 99.7 percent of all employer firms, employed half of all private sector employees, paid 44 percent of total U.S. private payroll, were 52 percent home-based, and they produced thirteen times more patents per employee than

---

1   Bureau of Labor Statistics website October 7, 2011 statistical release found at http://data.bls.gov/cgi-bin/print.pl/news.release/empsit.a.htm

2   http://www.bls.gov/web/laus/laumstrk.htm

3   http://web.sba.gov/faqs/faqIndexAll.cfm?areaid=24

large firms.[1] Clearly, we need more of them!

Creating a new business requires capital. Even setting up a lawn-cutting service requires acquiring mowers, edgers, and trucks. A new nail salon requires money for chairs and foot-soaking tubs.

Most banks do not lend amounts smaller than $50,000 to businesses.

How do we, as a society, create a source of loan funds for emerging small businesses that do not fit the large lenders' criteria?

One answer is microlending. Microlending refers to the practice of lending small amounts of money to qualified entrepreneurs and small businesses. Found in San Francisco, San Antonio, New Orleans, Charlotte, and many other U.S. cities, microlenders exist for the sole purpose of helping small businesses get started.

Often offered by a nonprofit organization established just for this purpose, the lender has different business terms for the borrower to meet than those of the typical multistate bank. The first difference is that the microlender does not intend to repackage the loan along with others and resell it on Wall Street. Instead, the loan is small, is for a short duration, and is owned and managed locally.

The second difference is in the criteria used to qualify for the loan. As a society we have gone from an era when loans were given based on the borrower's character, family reputation, and track record, to an era today where loan committees approve loans based on credit ratings and the number of times folks were late paying on their credit card.

1   http://web.sba.gov/faqs/faqIndexAll.cfm?areaid=24

What has been lost is the very important measure of character, and one's ability to learn from past mistakes—something neighbors, fellow business people, and friends are in
a better position to assess and which, until several decades
ago, played a larger role in the loan-making process than it
appears to play today.

In discussions I have had with active members of
these microlending organizations, a common theme has
emerged—that "it takes a village to raise a new business."
This village is created by a requirement *attached to the loan*
that the borrower be adopted, trained, and supervised by
lending-agency staff and sponsors. These are individuals who have already proven themselves in the world of
finance and business. Microlending is not just a financial
transaction—it is economic and human development.

There are many microlenders in the United States,
including the Michael Scott Mater Foundation in Charlotte,
North Carolina, which is deeply committed to borrower
education and training as a condition of granting a loan.

The Opportunity Fund (www.opportunityfund.org/)
is another organization that provides microlending in the
U.S. This organization operates in many states, and has
an on-line application process. The vast majority of loans
are between $1,000 and $10,000.[1] Another well-known
microlender is AccionUSA (www.accionusa.org), which
has loaned more than $119 million in more than 19,000
microloans since its inception in 1991.[2] These two organi-

---

1   http://www.opportunityfund.org/about/small-business-loans/mi-
     crofinance

2   http://www.accionusa.org/ lower left of main page

zations joined forces recently to hold a Microfinance USA conference in order to educate the public about the benefits of microlending. The two organizations report "a business survival rate twice the national average, repayment rates that rival those of mainstream lenders, and a boost in local job creation for each loan provided."[1]

We do not have to act as if economic matters are out of our control. We can approach our friends about starting a local fund for microinvesting, or ask existing microlending funds how we can help them with outreach and marketing their resources in our communities. We can also deposit some of our own money with microlenders so they can expand their good works while saving our economy. The record shows that we are likely to earn a higher rate of return than we currently do, while creating a stronger local economy.

We are not powerless. We can come together and each put our money where our mouth is. Our communities will be better for it.

---

1   "Microfinance USA Conference to Ignite Action for Increased Microfinance Services in the United States." 5/9/11. Accessed 6/22/11. http://www.opportunityfund.org/news/press-release

Create the New Capitalism with Old Ideas and New Tools

In the past few years, our once diverse and decentralized banking system has experienced dramatic change. Three out of every four dollars entrusted to banks are now held by just six institutions (sometimes referred to as the "too-big-to-fail banks").[1,2] This change has significant implications on your family's future, particularly in the area of job creation in your community.

These six institutions focus on profitable large commercial loans, consumer accounts, and credit cards. They approve only around one in six loan requests from small businesses[3]—if you want a loan to start or grow a small business, you won't find a welcome mat there. The banks eager for your business are those that control the other one out of every four dollars—the 7,000 community banks.[4] Get it? Six banks control three-quarters of the money—7,000 control the rest. In recent years, unlike the big banks, these community banks have approved one out of every two

---

1   http://www.fdic.gov/regulations/resources/cbi/report/cbi-full.pdf

2   Bank of America Corp. (BAC), Citigroup Inc. (C), Goldman Sachs Group Inc., (GS)JPMorgan Chase & Co. (JPM), Morgan Stanley and Wells Fargo & Co (WFC). List from Bloomberg Press May 10, 2013

3   http://smallbusiness.foxbusiness.com/finance-accounting/2013/05/14/how-technology-is-boosting-small-business-lending/

4   http://www.icba.org/files/ICBASites/PDFs/cbfacts.pdf

small business loan requests.[1] However, there is a wrinkle.

Close your eyes and visualize a small business. How does it compare to the following definition of a "small" business, which is the one used by both lenders and the Small Business Administration: construction—$35 million annual receipts; manufacturing—between 500 and 1,000 employees; retail trade—around $7 million in annual receipts.[2]

The word *small* is misleading. We need another term to get to what I'm talking about. There is one. The technical term for a business with less than one million dollars in sales is *microbusiness*. Typically, such a business employs five people or less. There are 27 million microbusinesses in the United States.[3] Almost all of them need capital to get up and running; once running, they need funds in order to expand.

When the people controlling 75 percent of all the lendable money turn down five out of every six loan requests, and the most cooperative banks with the least amount of money to lend turn down one out of every two requests, what does the future of job creation through new businesses look like? Grim.

Communities need to fix this in order to create a better future.

The most common source of money to start up new businesses comes from family and friends. One fun exam-

1 http://smallbusiness.foxbusiness.com/finance-account-ing/2013/05/14/how-technology-is-boosting-small-business-lending/

2 http://www.sba.gov/content/guide-size-standards

3 http://boss.blogs.nytimes.com/2012/11/07/the-joys-and-dangers-of-owning-a-microbusiness/

ple is Mr. Jonathan Swift, an Irish Episcopalian priest, best known as the author of *Gulliver's Travels*. Faced with Ireland's overwhelming poverty in the 1700s, he organized an investment fund created by parish donors. This fund was loaned out in small amounts to other parishioners to help them break the cycle of poverty by starting a business and employing their fellows.[1] This is an early version of a "hand up," not a "hand out."

Fast forward three centuries, and you find the modern equivalent—funding entrepreneurs on the internet.

In the world of business, the on-line solicitation of investors is known as crowdfunding. This concept received a huge boost when both political parties came together to pass, and President Obama signed, the Jumpstart Our Business Start-Ups Act.[2] Microbusiness owners post their market analysis and business plan—and blindly solicit investors. Interested parties can make a loan, or receive an equity interest in the new company, or take a percentage ownership in some asset like a truck or real estate. In some cases, investors can combine all three.

The best-known site is Kickstarter, which started in April of 2009. Just four years later, more than $381 million had been invested in new businesses! On February 9, 2012, two projects (a charging dock for an iPhone and a computer game) tied for the honor of raising more than a million dollars in investment through Kickstarter in a single day.[3]

1   Samuel Johnson's "Life of Swift": JaffeBros. From his *Lives of the Poets*

2   http://www.gpo.gov/fdsys/pkg/BILLS-112hr3606enr/pdf/BILLS-112hr3606enr.pdf

3   http://en.wikipedia.org/wiki/Kickstarter

Not all projects are this size. Two teachers in Billings, Montana, had an idea to create party dinnerware that locked a bowl onto a dinner plate so that people attending a reception could carry both without spilling. They created a business plan, determined they needed a minimum of $20,000, posted their solicitation, and in a few minutes had their first $100. A few days later, they had secured 300 investors, meeting their goal of $20,000.[1]

If you Google "crowdfunding business start-ups," you will find more than ten pages of links to explore.

We can create a better future filled with many new jobs if we study role models in history like Father Swift, update our view of how the world of big money is really working, and adapt to new tools.

---

1   http://billingsgazette.com/business/billings-partners-use-crowd-funding-to-launch-their-dinnerware-venture/article_904cce30-8000-598e-97a6-6623ea6569c7.html

Smart Local Investors
Do Well and Do Good

I love it when I find examples of places where one can do well financially while doing good in the community.

This phrase refers to situations where you can invest money or talent, earn a handsome rate of return or a decent living, and make the world a better place for your children—all at the same time. You would be doing good, and your investment in the community would result in financial gain.

If you took $1,000 and invested it in a certificate of deposit in any of the three largest banks in America today, you would earn one percent or less on your money—and have to pay income tax on that gain.[1, 2, 3]

Take the same $1,000 and put it in a secure government bond mutual fund, and your return might get as high as two percent in today's market.[4]

However, if you invested in your own community, you could earn an after-tax return of between five and seven percent.

---

1   http://fundresearch.fidelity.com/mutual-funds/category-performance-daily-pricing-yields/BNDIDX

2   https://online.citibank.com/US/JRS/pands/detail.do?ID=SvgCDs

3   https://www.bankofamerica.com/deposits/bank-account-interest-rates.go

4   http://fundresearch.fidelity.com/mutual-funds/category-performance-daily-pricing-yields/BNDIDX

The story actually starts several years ago with the John Deere Corporation.

In the windy Great Plains, new wind power was the first renewable energy source to be competitive with newly constructed coal or nuclear plants. Investors who wanted to lease land on which to locate windmills approached farmers. The farmers would be able to continue farming around the towers—just as they do around electric distribution towers. Once the farmers understood the economics of the proposed deal, they wanted to become investors as well. Familiar with John Deere as a seller and financier of large farm equipment, the farmers approached the company and asked to borrow money to invest in wind farms.

John Deere investigated the projects, and concluded that they would be profitable and grant a measure of economic security to their farmer-customers. These customers would likely use some of their profits to buy new farm equipment from Deere. John Deere agreed to become a third-party investor in renewable energy, and an industry was born.[1]

The economic model also works in urban areas where nonprofits such as schools and libraries can capitalize on the sunshine on their rooftops. These institutions have been at a disadvantage when installing renewable energy because they cannot take advantage of the same tax incentives enjoyed by for-profit companies. Without those tax incentives, taxpayer-supported school systems have to shell out more than for-profit entities do to install solar energy systems.

---

1   http://money.cnn.com/2007/09/05/news/companies/deere_wind/index.htm

Building on the John Deere experience, entrepreneurs have now figured out that they can set up limited partnerships where local folks can invest in local projects. These local for-profit limited partnerships buy solar, wind, and geothermal energy equipment, and place it on the rooftops or adjacent property of schools, libraries, jails, and other public entities. These investments now work under the same tax code rules that govern the public utilities—and can be just as profitable.

The terms of the deal typically involve the school or library leasing its rooftop to the investor group for a period of years. The private investors earn a handsome rate of return for five or six years from the sale of electricity and by claiming various tax benefits. They then *donate the system to the nonprofit*, and the private investor thus receives another benefit—a tax deduction for their charitable contribution. This arrangement allows the nonprofits to enjoy significantly reduced energy bills for the remaining twenty-five or so years of the project. Both parties win. In addition, public health improves because of reduced pollution.

Another source of pride for local investors is that the local economy also wins big. The skilled labor needed to install this equipment is employed on local projects instead of at some distant coal mine or on a well-drilling rig in the middle of the ocean.

Several existing companies are putting these ideas into action.

On the West Coast, SolarMosaic[1] has so successfully matched investors with local projects that *Bloomberg Press*,

---

1   https://joinmosaic.com/

The Wall Street Journal, The New York Times and *Fortune* magazine have all given the company favorable reviews.[1]

A second example is The Appalachian Institute for Renewable Energy (AIRE), located in Boone, North Carolina. Using start-up funds from the Kendeda Fund, which supported two years' worth of preparation, AIRE has developed legal templates and economic calculations that assist local investors in forming for-profit businesses that develop community renewable energy for nonprofits, civic organizations, churches, and municipalities.[2] Working with what they call "empathetic investors," they have successfully completed several prototype projects and are now eagerly seeking new projects.

So, if you are scared of Wall Street, tired of paying high taxes, want to create local employment, and clean up the environment—all while earning a great rate of return—you have reason to be optimistic about our future. Pick up the phone, call one of these organizations, and put your money where your heart is.

---

1   https://joinmosaic.com/
2   http://aire-nc.org/brochure/

Create Jobs
Without Using Money

According to national statistics, approximately one in seven potential workers in the United States is unable to find paid work.[1] This contributes to rising crime, domestic violence, and mental health issues.

Critical social services programs have been cut because of declining tax revenues. Private donations to organizations that help the less fortunate have also dropped over the past few years.[2] The net effect is that we have more people needing help and fewer charity dollars available. These are hard times.

Fortunately, it is possible to jump-start a local economy without using U. S. currency—by using a creative, non-cash-based solution that can put people to work. It is a barter system, trading work for goods, or work for work, with no cash involved. New software makes implementing this system easy, even at the local level.

To make the system work, an organization sets up a computer program for a "barter exchange." This works like Craigslist or matchmaker websites. It connects unemployed

---

1   http://www.bls.gov/news.release/empsit.t15.htm (this is called the Bureau of Labor Statistics U-6 rate)

2   http://www.nonprofitquarterly.org/philanthropy/2766-charitable-giving-falls-again.html

willing workers to folks or organizations who need to have work done but do not have the funds to pay the worker. Instead of receiving cash, the worker is compensated by receiving either a certificate with value (could be a gift card) or items of value such as food or a night of shelter. They can take this credit and spend it, just like cash, with other members of the barter exchange who have committed to accept barter and have posted goods or services they will trade.

Imagine a soup-kitchen charity that needs a supermarket's surplus vegetables picked up each Monday evening. It is matched with an unemployed person who has a truck that is refrigerated, or has the capacity to carry large boxes with ice in them. The charity gets the food, the grocery gets a tax deduction for making a charitable gift, and the truck driver gets a redeemable coupon that she can trade for other things—furniture at Goodwill or food from the local food bank, for example. The driver gets her self-esteem back, and the food winds up feeding people rather than rotting in a landfill.

Instead of removing wealth from the charity system, charity recipients can use barter to become contributors to the system. The pool of help available to the community expands, while the for-profit company increases its bottom line!

Barter systems enable direct trades such as, "I will take Mrs. Jones to the doctor in exchange for free groceries from the food bank." The trade can involve creation of credits that are portable; for example, "I get four credits for taking Mrs. Jones to the doctor, which I can apply toward having Mr. Smith (another labor-exchange member) fix my rotten front steps." The only requirement is that everyone involved be a member of the system and agree in advance to play by the rules.

There are hundreds of systems like this working in the U.S. right now. Some involve exchanges with for-profit organizations like motels, which can trade empty rooms with charities, thus creating emergency overnight shelter for battered women.

One good example of this is a charity called Resources for Human Development in Philadelphia. They bartered $1.5 million worth of goods and services without a penny of U.S. currency changing hands. The charity got labor it needed, the charity recipients who could work did so, the barter workers got value in exchange for their labor, and the community safety net expanded. You can learn more about this at www.equaldollars.org.[1]

The for-profit sector has used this same barter technique for years. According to the International Reciprocal Trade Association, annual barter transactions exceeded $12 billion in cash value in 2009/2010.[2]

The Internal Revenue Service recognizes barter exchanges as a legitimate economic activity and has simple rules in place, just as if the workers were paid in cash.[3] Surprisingly, barter income can result in a family becoming eligible for

---

1   http://www.rhd.org/News/11-06-22/RHD_s_Equal_Dollars_opens_
      new_community_food_bank_at_Unitarian_Society_of_German-
      town.aspx

2   http://www.facebook.com/pages/International-Reciprocal-Trade-
      Association/111400412243502

3   http://www.irs.gov/taxtopics/tc420.html

an Earned Income Tax Credit.[1] The tax reporting require-
ments are easily managed by the specialized computer
systems that the sponsoring agency installs.

In these highly politicized times when agreeable solutions are hard to find, barter does not require government
action.

---

1   http://www.irs.gov/individuals/article/0,,id=96466,00.html

Create Local Jobs with Gift Cards

With the economy in the dumps, and faith in national decision-makers at an all-time low, is it time to take local action to create jobs and protect local employers? Can a community do well by doing good?

Some communities think they can, and they are proving it. In these communities, entrepreneurs and local small businesses, in partnership with a small local or regional bank or credit union, have created local gift cards.

These cards are "branded" with the identity of the organization that set up the program, and are used to buy goods and services only from locally owned businesses—not the big-box stores and businesses that ship money out of the community.

Case in point: in Dane County, Wisconsin, a group of local business people started the Dane County Buy Local gift card program several years ago. They persuaded a group of locally owned businesses to agree to both sell and accept the cards; then they persuaded the local bank to create and process them.

The cards are just like any other debit card, but they have a "Dane Buy Local" logo. It took only two months from initial agreement on the plan to get the first cards into customers' hands.

Today, the cards are available at, and accepted by, 538 member businesses. Learn more about the program at www.danebuylocal.com.

In Chattanooga, Tennessee, the Buy It Downtown program began in 2007 as a project of Buy it Local, LLC, in cooperation with a local downtown partnership. Initially, a group of sixteen businesses agreed to participate by selling and redeeming the Buy It Downtown cards. This local gift card now has more than ninety participating merchants. It has had a multimillion-dollar impact on the local economy, directing hundreds of thousands of dollars to each of the participating merchants.

In its first year these cards facilitated more than $100,000 in business to local retailers and service providers, and then experienced double- and triple-digit annual growth, even throughout the economic recession. Business owners realized that the customers often used the cards to pay for only a portion of a purchase, leveraging an additional 40 percent in business beyond the face value of the cards to the local business, not to mention the impact on the community resulting from recycling dollars locally.

Since its initial program development, Buy it Local has created Buy It*Cards, a program and system it provides to other local areas so they can create their own local gift card program. They can then track the results on its unique web-based system. Learn more about Chattanooga's program at www.buyitdowntown.com and Buy It*Cards at www.buyitcards.com.

This kind of program has a significant impact on the local economy, because each dollar spent in a community business is more likely to stay within that community. For example, a local landscape company buys a new mower from a locally owned company; the seller of the mower buys printing from the locally owned print shop; the print-shop owner buys locally grown flowers for his wife from the local florist—and they all have a bit more to put into the church collection basket or to hire their unemployed neighbor.

Let's use Mr. Jones as an example. If Santa Claus flew over Mr. Jones' town during a time of high unemployment, scattered money all around, and each of the unemployed (including Mr. Jones) put that cash under their beds, they might feel richer, but Mr. Jones would still be unemployed.

If they took their money and bought products from a foreign land or a big-box store, they may have changed that wealth to a different form, but Mr. Jones would still be unemployed.

But if Santa dropped off branded gift cards to be spent at locally owned and operated businesses, members of the community would buy these businesses' products. The resulting increase in consumer demand would mean their friends and neighbors might be hired by these businesses. In other words, increasing local economic demand could result in employment for Mr. Jones.

These "buy local" gift cards are more useful than cards issued by a single store because they can be used in many different kinds of stores, ranging from the local dry cleaners to locally owned art galleries, pharmacies, tax preparers— any local business that accepts a Visa card.

One of the measures of the health of a local economy is how many times a dollar changes hands before it leaves the area. The more money shipped out of a community, the poorer the local economy. Buying locally raises the number of times a dollar turns over in a community — and local gift cards help that happen.

Our future is in our control far more than many of us think. There are many ways towns and communities can take control of their futures again.

Band Together to Create Jobs

Just about the time the South's furniture and textile economy collapsed, so did the steel and chemical-based industrial economy of Cleveland, Ohio.

Cleveland used to supply much of the steel for the Detroit automobile industry. Car and truck sales in the United States have fallen by one third over the past thirteen years, and a significant portion of those sold are now made outside of Detroit. Almost half of all Cleveland's manufacturing jobs have vanished.[1] Hundreds of thousands of jobs have been lost forever.

After some years of struggle, leadership in Cleveland pioneered a very interesting role model of economic development which may be worth imitating.

A coalition of large nonprofit institutions began meeting to discuss what they could collectively do to fix things. The original community heavyweights included Case Western Reserve University, Cleveland Clinic, University Hospital, and Cleveland Foundation. The Board of Directors now includes leaders in many of the area's for-profit companies.[2] They decided to build local economic development from the ground up. Their goal was to create new for-profit companies

---

1   http://www.brookings.edu/~/ media/research/files/papers/2011/6/ manufacturing%20job%20loss/06_manufacturing_job_loss.pdf

2   Phone conversation Mr. John McMicken, CEO Evergreen Cooperative Corporation January 23, 2014

that would employ people in the neighborhoods hardest hit by the economic downturn. They named themselves the Evergreen Cooperative.

During planning discussions, they had three major insights:

First, they realized their institutions were major consumers. They did the math. Turns out, they spent more than $3 billion every year.[1] That's billion with a "B."

Second, the planners concluded that if they coordinated their purchases of some items, they could create and support substantial new local companies. These new companies could offer products for which large local demand already exists, as well as receive the supportive business training they needed.

Third, in response to a history of companies leaving the area, the planners decided that the companies they would start would be largely worker-owned and thus anchored in the community.

They focused on areas of the economy likely to grow significantly due to changing demographics or market trends. These included health care, the service industries to support an aging population, and the need for reliable food and energy supplies that do not contribute to environmental degradation. They were sensitive to this last issue because the Cuyahoga River, which flows through the center of town, had caught fire many times in past decades due to pollution.[2]

---

1   http://www.thenews.coop/article/ted-howard-reveals-success-behind-cleveland-model

2   http://clevelandhistorical.org/items/show/63#.Ut1v8hAo6Cg

So far, the Evergreen Cooperative has started three successful companies: a commercial laundry, a hydroponics vegetable producer, and an installer of energy conservation technology and solar energy in homes and businesses.

The laundry was started in 2009 and has earned a LEED Silver certificate, a status granted to buildings that are extraordinarily energy efficient. It currently has forty-two full-time employees, and is handling six million pounds of commercial laundry each year from health care and hospitality institutions.

The hydroponics company occupies 3.25 acres of growing area and has the capacity to produce 3 million heads of lettuce and 300,000 pounds of herbs each year.[1] Production is on track to reach that goal. As of January 2014, it had a payroll of twenty-six full-time employees, and is projected to grow to around forty.[2] You can see a wonderful video about that effort at http://evergreencooperatives.com/.

A fun insight occurred during the evolution of the energy company, now called Evergreen Energy Solutions. The weather is too cold and harsh during Cleveland's five-month winter to safely crawl around on rooftops installing solar collectors. Of course, as soon as the cold weather arrives, potential customers wake up to the need to save on expensive heating energy. The solution? As cold weather approaches, the energy company takes its workers off the roofs and puts them to work installing energy conserva-

---

1   http://www.greenhousegrower.com/business-management/green-
     city-growers-is-largest-urban-food-co-op-in-u-s/6/
2   Phone conversation Mr. John McMicken, CEO Evergreen Coopera-
     tive Corporation January 23, 2014

tion systems inside buildings, including rapidly-growing numbers of retrofit LED installations in commercial facilities, thus ensuring year-round work. They employ sixteen workers and have a significant backlog of work.[1]

Each of the new companies is a minimum 80 percent owned by the vested employees. A holding company supervised by the Board of Directors owns the rest. Employee shareholders actively participate in committees that seek to improve day-to-day operations at the three companies.

Seventeen other cities have efforts underway to duplicate Evergreen's success.[2]

Cities and towns can learn many lessons from Cleveland's Evergreen Cooperative. Key behaviors to emulate are the way leaders in prominent and substantial organizations (both elected and private sector) cooperated, created a vision of a sustainable future, and changed their collective behavior in order to achieve their goals. Instead of doing nothing and becoming victims of circumstances, they realized that the future is something they could shape.

---

1   Phone conversation Mr. John McMicken, CEO Evergreen Cooperative Corporation January 23, 2014

2   http://www.thenews.coop/article/ted-howard-reveals-success-behind-cleveland-model 7 minutes into the video

Employee Ownership Yields Big Dividends

Suppose you are unemployed and have a family to feed. After months of looking, you receive offers for two jobs and have to choose between them. Both are with new companies founded by neighborhood entrepreneurs. One offers a standard wage, regular hours, and so forth. The other offers the same things but adds the requirement that all employees own shares of stock in the new company. Over the years, which company will have contributed to making your family economically secure? Which one would you enjoy working at the most? Which one will have strengthened the local economy?

The bottom line is that when employees own significant stock in a company and participate in its management, the company's sales and payroll grow 30 percent faster over ten years than if the employees do not own a piece of the action.[1]

When we compare employee-owned companies to publicly held companies of similar size and age in the same industries, the employee-owned companies are 10 percent more profitable,[2] wages are 5 to 12 percent higher,[3] and

---

1   http://www.nceo.org/articles/research-employee-ownership-corpo-
    rate-performance — see 2000 Rutgers study

2   "The ESOP Performance Puzzle in Public Companies," Fall 2006
    issue of the Journal of Employee Ownership Law and Finance

3   http://www.nceo.org/articles/research-employee-ownership-corpo-

retirement plan assets are 2.6 times greater.[1]

When it comes to layoffs, non-employee-owned companies lay off their workers at four times the rate of employee-owned companies.[2] In addition, unionized firms with significant employee ownership of shares have fewer strikes.[3] (After all, who wants to go on strike against themselves?) A Canadian study found that worker-owned economic enterprises of all sizes had a business failure rate roughly half that of non-worker-owned.[4]

I am not talking about companies where employees can buy a few shares of company stock in their retirement account. I am talking about large companies (including those publicly traded on the stock market) where employees own the majority of shares, and small companies of less than 40 employees who own all of the shares. In both of these cases, it is possible to establish what is sometimes called an "employee-owned culture." This results in improved company performance through structured meetings that mine the insights and input of the employees/owners.

While employee ownership stakes can be a significant factor in helping young or small companies survive, it also helps them achieve their growth potential. Examples

rate-performance See Kardas Study

1   http://www.nceo.org/articles/research-employee-ownership-corpo-rate-performance See Kardas study

2   http://www.esopassociation.org/docs/default-source/press-release-docs/here.pdf?sfvrsn=0

3   http://www.newyorkfed.org/research/staff_reports/sr347.pdf

4   http://www.ontario.coop/all_about_cooperatives/what_is_a_coop/why_do_coops_work

of companies that are majority employee-owned show up on "Forbes 100 Best Companies to Work For" lists. In fact, one in ten of the winners is majority-owned by employees.[1] These include Publix Supermarkets, Men's Wearhouse, and Proctor & Gamble.[2]

Another of the advantages for smaller businesses that involve employees in ownership is that these companies stay rooted where they are planted. If various forms of state and local incentives are used, those granting them (and facing re-election challenges) know that the company they are supporting will be more likely to survive and stick around if local workers own at least a part of the business.

Business incubators and business accelerators are wonderful economic development engines that have now spread all across the United States. Many are sponsored in part by local education institutions, others by municipal entities like cities or counties. However, I was surprised to find that of the approximately 1,100 surviving Incubators,[3] only a handful appear to focus on employee ownership.[4]

If your town is trying to improve its local economy, and has business incubators or other forms of sponsorship in new companies, you could clearly help us all out by introducing them to the facts outlined above. You can also tell them about the Ohio Employee Ownership Center at Kent State University, and the National Center for Employee

1   http://www.nceo.org/articles/research-employee-ownership-corpo-
     rate-performance
2   http://www.nceo.org/great-employee-owned-places-work/id/34/
3   https://www.nbia.org/about_nbia/
4   Derived from several phone conversations with experts who could
     not name but two or three.

Ownership in Oakland, California, both of which have much more information available.

Part of the DNA of the United States is the admiration for small-business entrepreneurs who "make it" by starting in a garage, hiring some friends, and ramping up and hiring more. Creating new employment is now more than a talking point. It is a mission vital to the future of our families and country. The data clearly shows that sharing ownership of the new companies with the workforce supports that mission.

Energize Local Economies Through Creative Deconstruction

There is a way to use charity to create jobs and improve the community.

I love the title of the effort, "Creative Deconstruction."

In many older neighborhoods, there are houses or businesses that are abandoned or damaged. They have become places that parents warn their children to avoid. Sometimes the buildings attract critters like skunks, occasionally of the human variety. Neighbors begin to petition for the building to be torn down or fixed up. Often the building owner does not have the money to do either, so the problem sits and grows worse. Broken windows lead to water damage and mold, pipes freeze and leak, drywall is ruined. Overall, it ends up a mess.

Still, the building may contain items of value such as solid oak flooring, kitchen cabinets, or a stair railing worn smooth by generations of little bottoms. Others might have usable toilets or sinks, generously-sized tubs with fancy legs, light fixtures, air-conditioning units, and even the boards or iron beams that make up the frame of the building. They may also have marble fireplaces, fancy mantles, or reusable exterior bricks.

Often the city or county goes through the expensive legal process of condemning the property, seizing title, and then billing the taxpayer to knock it down and haul it to the landfill. This is a painful process for everyone, especially for the owner who might become a pauper as a result. This is a step backward from an economic development standpoint.

A better route is the use of creative deconstruction. The local government works with the building owner, and arranges with an organization (the creative deconstructer) to have the building torn down. Independent of any other costs, this technique allows the owner to donate the salvageable materials to a charity and get a tax deduction.

The Institute for Local Self Reliance, a national organization that educates communities on successful models of local economic development, began working in the area of creative deconstruction fifteen years ago. This organization is a treasure. With the help of the Institute, several hundred communities have now started their own creative deconstruction programs.[1] These have been so successful that the U.S. Dept. of Housing and Urban Development (HUD) now encourages the technique in government-funded neighborhood redevelopment. HUD will fund or help fund new company start-ups in this arena.[2]

The hundreds of groups that operate these programs confidentially state some rather surprising facts. First, the building owner often saves money rather than spending it to bulldoze the property and, additionally, gets to keep the land. Second, in Portland, Oregon, the ReBuilding Center has learned that deconstructing a building creates

---

1   http://www.ilsr.org/westmoreland-deconstruction-case-study/
2   http://www.ilsr.org/12857/

six-to-eight jobs compared to standard demolition.[1] Third, students who volunteer to help can learn a great deal about the building trade. Fourth, the donation of recycled building materials and fixtures often helps low-income families realize their home improvement dreams. This effort benefits everyone.

As mentioned earlier, for-profit companies do the actual creative deconstruction (not bulldozing), but they collaborate in advance with charities that accept the reusable salvaged materials for resale. This allows the charity to maintain focus on its store without having to manage a construction company. A good example of this is The ReUse People, a franchise system that has a location in Durham, North Carolina. This franchise collaborates with nonprofits while keeping a clear eye on its own bottom line.[2]

Habitat for Humanity of Charlotte's ReStore operation has a program where the owner of nice looking reusable kitchen cabinets can get a free professional opinion as to the merits and tax implications of having the cabinets carefully removed and donated for resale.[3] After the donation is made and the donor receives the tax benefit, Habitat sells the items and proceeds are recycled to help build more Habitat homes.

The North East Community Action Corporation of St. Louis, Missouri, has a good deconstruction manual describing detailed, experience-based comparisons of the cost and

1   http://rebuildingcenter.org/deconstruction-services/about/

2   http://thereusepeople.org/locations#NorthCarolina

3   http://www.charlotterestore.org/programs/deconstruction

benefits to the landlord of the deconstruct model.[1]

Despite this magnificent track record, in many parts of the country the old ways still prevail. The Institute for Local Self Reliance estimates that only one out of 250 abandoned homes is deconstructed. The rest are simply bulldozed at great expense.[2]

A waste of waste.

Much of our nation, particularly the older communities, are suffering both a loss of jobs and of hope. We can fix this by imitating the successful efforts of both for-profit and nonprofit organizations. Sometimes it is not just physical property that is recycled and restored. With proper guidance, local leadership can also recycle lives damaged by financial loss.

---

1   http://www.iowacommunityaction.org/Resources/NECAC%20Final%20Report_FINAL.pdf

2   http://www.ilsr.org/12857/

Incubators Support Local Entrepreneurs and Improve Communities

There are two significant facts that will severely affect our nation's future unless solutions are put into place. The first is the number of unemployed, which depending on the definition used is estimated to be between one in eight or one in twenty potential workers.[1] The second is that many newly created jobs do not have the same level of pay as the jobs that have vanished. Consequently, real income has declined in working-aged households, from $63,500 in 2000 to $53,657 in 2014.[2] Ouch!

Clearly, creating well-paying jobs needs to be a priority.

One technique is to create business incubators, entities where new companies get additional support from advisors and leaders of more mature companies. They work. Nationally, only 49 percent of unsheltered new businesses survive their first five years,[3] but *87 percent of incubator graduates are still in business after five years.*[4]

Incubators are very cost-effective. A careful study was done comparing the impact of several models of widely

---

1. http://www.bls.gov/news.release/empsit.t15.htm (this is called the Bureau of Labor Statistics U-6 rate)
2. https://research.stlouisfed.org/fred2/series/MEHOINUSA672N
3. http://efactory.missouristate.edu/BusinessIncubator/About.htm
4. http://efactory.missouristate.edu/BusinessIncubator/About.htm

used job creation techniques. Non-incubator investments produced one job for each $3,306 spent. Business incubators created one job for an average investment of $180.[1]

As I researched the history of the nation's 1,100 surviving incubators, I began to see a formula for incubator failure and another for incubator success.

The formula for failure was to take some underused space, often in a part of town that needed a boost, but often far from office supply stores, computer technical support, and nice places to eat. Then staff it with competent people who could teach business subjects like accounting and taxes, but who themselves had never been entrepreneurs. Next, open it to all interested parties without screening and place them under some kind of Board of Directors that has to answer to municipal authorities, which results in an incubator with a risk-averse power structure. Finally, try to make the facility self-supporting too quickly. Places like this fail both their sponsors and their clients; they usually close down.[2]

The flip side of this is a recipe for success. You start by assembling a carefully screened set of emerging entrepreneurs and ask them what kinds of support they need to start or grow their desired company. Then you deliver what they ask for.

Sometimes an entrepreneur doesn't need space because the new company works out of a home garage, but they

1   http://www.nbia.org/resource_library/works/files/EDA_study_PR_FINAL.pdf. I took the max and min costs of job created and derived an average cost.

2   http://startupflorida.blogspot.com/2009/01/top-5-reasons-why-tech-incubators-fail.html

may need access to the president of a larger company for mentoring. The most successful incubators are staffed by successful entrepreneurs, whose primary contributions are recruiting talented leaders to act as mentors and coaches. They also facilitate active and supportive participation from Small Business Assistance Centers, Chambers of Commerce, and local governments.

High-performing incubators start with an inventory of their service area's assets, aspirations, and weaknesses. They identify sectors of community needs that can be satisfied by successful local businesses. One incubator team leader told me they were puzzling over the perceived net impact on the local economy of a rapidly aging population that may require more taxpayer support. Then they realized there would be a real market for retirement homes, home-nursing companies, specialty pharmacies, taxis, and a host of other support services. This is now a highly successful business-development arena.

The world of entrepreneurial facilitation requires constant adjustment as circumstances change. In a few areas, the word *incubator* has a bad connotation because it has come to mean low-cost real estate offering fledgling businesses some operating space without much else in the way of support. Some leaders in the job creation movement now feel that their point of highest advantage is working with established companies to help them reach their full potential, and they want to escape the negative local "incubator" brand.

In Louisville, Kentucky, the Chamber of Commerce operates EnterpriseCorp, which supports the region's entrepreneurial ecosystem. It has partnered with other local organizations to create what they call the High Impact Portfolio devoted to identifying existing small and mid-sized businesses with significant growth potential. After surviving a demanding screening process, a business is offered planning expertise, mentoring, expert consulting, and other assistance from companies in the region selected for their potential to make a specific contribution. There are 170 companies in this group, with annual revenues total-ling $2.7 billion. Since beginning the Portfolio, and with the assistance of the Portfolio network of local mentors, these companies have invested $500 million in their own growth, have grown 30 percent a year, and have created 3,600 jobs since 2005.[1] EnterpriseCorp's annual budget is less than $100,000.

More information is on the website of the National Business Incubator Association.

---

1   http://www.greaterlouisville.com/EnterpriseCORP/Services/
     HighImpactProgram/

Creating

an Economically

Sustainable

Local Food Supply

We Need to Have a Food Fight

When I scan the trends that will shape our future, I find several that pose moral issues that create tension with some definitions of "progress." In some ways, these issues seem designed to challenge us to examine basic assumptions about the society we have created and the kind of future we want.

In the health-care arena, doctors are pointing us toward some statistics that expose several unusual epidemics underway.

When you hear the word *epidemic*, you might think of a communicable disease like measles, polio, HIV, or cholera. In these cases, people get sick because they contract bacteria or viruses that take root in their bodies. While sick, they can pass the disease along to others. We address these diseases by quarantining the patient, administering antibiotics or other drugs, instituting widespread vaccinations, and so on.

There is another type of epidemic. The diseases of this type of epidemic are spreading rapidly through society but not by spreading germs to one another. Examples include obesity (up 200 percent since 1990),[1] autism (up 600 percent over the last twenty years),[2] and diabetes (up 400 percent

---

1   http://www.americashealthrankings.org/all/obesity
2   http://blog.autismspeaks.org/2010/10/22/got-questions-answers-to-your-questions-from-the-autism-speaks%E2%80%99-science-staff-2/

since 1980[1] and expected to double again by 2025).[2] These are all very expensive epidemics. They are growing because some underlying circumstances of our lives have changed that harm public health, increase unemployment, and raise the need for taxpayer support of the damaged citizen.

Part of the cause behind the explosions in these illnesses can be traced to changes in our food supply, which we can fix if we have the political will.

Cattle used to graze in pastures and eat grass rich in good nutrients. The meat from those cattle (loaded with those nutrients) fed our families and thus benefited human health.

Over time farmers realized that cattle grow faster, and more profitably, if they eat grass for nine or ten months but then are penned up for the last three or four months of their life. While they are penned, 95 percent of their diet (pay attention—this is important) consists of grains like corn and soy instead of grass.[3] They gain more weight more quickly—and more profitably.

Here is the problem—if we use "modern" methods to raise beef, we contribute to a decline in public health.

This can be illustrated by looking at changes in the nutrients found in meat since the 1960s, specifically the omega-6 to omega-3 ratio. Think of it like the amount of salt and pepper you put on a steak. Too much of one or the other is not a good thing. You want the right proportion.

---

1   http://www.cdc.gov/chronicdisease/resources/publications/aag/images/2011/new-cases-diabetes-adults-chart.gif

2   http://www.uclahealth.org/body.cfm?id=502&action=detail&ref=22

3   http://www.factory-farming.com/beef_production.html

Omega-3s are special kinds of fats that are beneficial to you. The list of good things they do is astonishing: they lower cholesterol, reduce rheumatoid arthritis, reduce depression, reduce ADHD, and protect against Alzheimer's and dementia.[1] In addition, they are thought to reduce inflammation, increase brain activity, and protect against stroke.[2]

Omega-6s, on the other hand, are good for you only up to a point, after which they become harmful. The key to a healthy diet is for you to eat *one* omega-6 for every *one* omega-3.[3] Our modern American diet contains around *sixteen* omega-6s for every *one* omega-3.[4]

Corn and soy create far more omega-6 than omega-3 in cattle. Grain-fed beef has a ratio of fourteen omega-6s for every one omega-3. Grass-fed beef has a ratio of 2:1—much better for you.[5]

This plays out in public policy where under current law farmers who raise corn and soy will get federal subsidies of around $45 billion over the next ten years.[6] Farmers who raise grass-fed beef get nothing. Taxpayers are subsidizing a food system that increases illness.

---

1   http://www.webmd.com/healthy-aging/omega-3-fatty-acids-fact-sheet

2   http://www.hsph.harvard.edu/nutritionsource/omega-3/

3   http://www.ncbi.nlm.nih.gov/pubmed/12442909

4   http://www.ncbi.nlm.nih.gov/pubmed/12442909

5   http://eatlocalgrown.com/article/grass-fed-vs-feedlot-beef-difference.html

6   http://www.washingtonpost.com/lifestyle/food/farm-bill-why-dont-taxpayers-subsidize-the-foods-that-are-better-for-us/2014/02/14/d7642a3c-9434-11e3-84e1-27626c5ef5fb_story.html

You can help your own family by reducing the amount of omega-6s they eat. The main culprits are soybean and corn oil, often used in bottled salad dressings and store-baked goods, as well as in most junk food.[1] Cut back on those, and you will make your family healthier.

Solving this problem will not be easy, because it lives in the zone where profit and common good collide. Perhaps those favoring lowering health-care costs can share a cup of coffee with those trying to lower taxes and find common ground. It is a place to start.

Local institutions and public servants (both elected and volunteers) can help by removing junk food from public institution food service and vending machines, taxing unhealthy sugar-laden drinks, and encouraging the local agriculture extension service to work with the Chamber of Commerce to strengthen the food-based sector of your local economy by re-use of both land and old factory buildings in creative ways. You will find examples of success stories already in place somewhere in America in subsequent chapters.

---

1   http://authoritynutrition.com/optimize-omega-6-omega-3-ratio/

The Link Between Community Death Rate and Making Local Food-Producing Jobs

Recent data published by the Central Intelligence Agency (CIA) shows that the United States ranks #42 in life expectancy in the world (behind Japan at #3, Sweden at #12, France at #15, and Ireland at #27).[1] There are many reasons for this, ranging from the way health care is structured to the amount of chemical pollution in the environment to how the illegal drug culture is managed. Few people think about the role of food—where it comes from and what is in it.

There are three surprising facts about food that almost no one knows—and they absolutely impact the life expectancy and health of you and yours—and the health of your local economy.

Start with this: British researchers studied 65,000 people over a seven-year period and found that people who ate seven portions of fruits or vegetables every day have a 42 percent lower death rate than those who ate four or fewer servings.[2] Studies by the Centers for Disease Control (CDC) show that only 11 percent of Americans eat that many.[3]

---

1   https://www.cia.gov/library/publications/the-world-factbook/ rankorder/2102rank.html

2   "Eat seven portions of fruit and vegetables a day to lower death"— http://medicalnewstoday.com/articles/274841.php

3   http://www.cncahealth.com/explore/learn/nutrition-food/declining-

A second interesting fact is that today's American fruits and veggies are missing a lot of vitamins and minerals that existed in those same crops fifty years ago. A woman eating a peach in 1951 got around *twenty-five* times more vitamin A than a woman today gets from eating a modern peach.[1] A 2004 study done at the University of Texas found that there were "reliable declines" in "protein, calcium, phosphorus, iron, B2, and vitamin C in crops grown in 1999 as compared to those grown in 1950.[2]

This decline seems particularly strong in compounds called phytochemicals (also known as phytonutrients). These substances occur naturally in food and give it color.[3] Very important to human health, phytochemicals fight prostate cancer, cataracts, macular degeneration, asthma, heart disease, and a host of other diseases. However, there are less phytochemicals in today's produce.[4]

Researchers theorized that these reductions in health-supporting ingredients were due to the creation of plant breeds developed for fast growth, better storage during shipping, pest resistance, and size of product.[5]

The third surprising fact is that between the time food is picked and the time it is eaten a lot of its nutrition vanishes. For example, the vitamin C in spinach is reduced by 75

nutrition-of-fruits-and-vegetables#.UzsWP1faHKd

1   Dirt Poor: Have Fruits and Vegetables Become Less Nutritious? Scientific American April 27, 2011

2   http://mannatechscience.org/files/file/Farm_to_Table.pdf

3   http://www.webmd.com/diet/phytonutrients-faq

4   http://www.ars.usda.gov/aboutus/docs.htm?docid=4142

5   Dirt Poor: Have Fruits and Vegetables Become Less Nutritious? Scientific American April 27, 2011

percent when refrigerated for seven days.[1] For supermarket "fresh" vegetables, the average distance traveled is around 1,500 miles,[2] and the time from farm to fork in the U.S. is fourteen days.[3] The future is now.

You can start to help both your family and your community by increasing the number of servings of fruits and vegetables up to the recommended seven per day. It is not that hard. Slice some bananas or apples into the breakfast cereal or add some chopped greens into the morning omelet. Pack some carrots and fresh fruit into those school lunches. For dinner, put broccoli or a sweet potato alongside the meat, add a salad, and you are there. Your life expectancy will soar.

When you plant your spring garden, buy seeds of older strains of fruits and vegetables. "Heirloom" veggies don't travel or store as well as modern hybrids, but they contain more nutrients and are a lot healthier for you.

You could get your food from something called Community Supported Agriculture (CSA). These small local food producers run their own agricultural businesses, growing food for specific customers who contract ahead to buy frequent (often weekly) shipments of food at optimal nutritional content. Customers know who grew the food, where it was grown, what variety it is, and the amount of chemicals and pesticides used, if any. The nutritional

1   http://www.healwithfood.org/nutritional-differences/frozen-fresh-vegetables.php

2   http://source.southuniversity.edu/farm-to-table-and-the-local-food-movement-49961.aspx

3   http://resourcespotlight.farmaid.org/2014/01/from-farm-to-fork-the-journey-of-food/

content of the food can easily be double that found in your supermarket produce because of the healthier varieties that are planted and less time spent traveling from farm to fork.

You can locate local food producers by going to www.localharvest.org, which will provide you a map of farmers in your area, and introduce you to CSAs who want your business. For example, in North Carolina, you can go to the Center for Environmental Farming Systems site at www.cefs.ncsu.edu for much valuable information.

Adapt Food Production
to Growing Population
and More Expensive Energy

Our food supply is enormously dependent on energy for making pesticides and fertilizer, processing, packaging, and transportation. In a rapidly growing world, this dependency will be a challenge.

Did you know that the population of the world is growing by the equivalent of the population of the United States every five years? In the next thirty years, the population of the earth will have expanded from 7 billion to 9 billion people—equal to an additional 6.5 United States of Americas.[1]

Think of the increased demand this will create for new supplies of food and energy. To those thoughts add the increased demand created by the improving standard of living in much of the world. For example, India and China currently have around one-third of the entire world's population.[2] Their average citizen currently uses less than one-tenth of the energy that a citizen of the U.S. uses.[3] However, per capita energy consumption in these emerging nations

---

1   World Population Prospects: The 2008 Revision Population Database http://esa.un.org/unpp/

2   Ibid.

3   See calculations below, derived from data found in the British Petroleum Company publication "Energy Outlook 2030" found at www.bp.com/...energy.../2030_energy_outlook_booklet.pdf

is expected to more than double in the next twenty years,[1] resulting in enormous new demands for energy.

Add the energy needs of this growing population (remember: 6.5 times the population of the U.S. in thirty years) to the anticipated doubling of per capita energy consumption in nations like India and China, and you get a demand for food and energy that will not be sustainable using today's resources and technologies. As demand increases, you will see a rapid rise in energy costs due to customers bidding for insufficient supplies. As servants of the public good, we can also examine the implications of this when shipping heavy food items, such as beef.

While researching this issue, I was surprised to learn that most U.S. farmers and cattlemen today work only part-time in these roles; they need "off-farm employment" to survive. The part-time cattleman presides over the cows' pregnancies and births, then ships the calves off to a place many miles away to be fattened up and slaughtered. The cattleman then tends to the mama cows to do it all over again. In the meantime, some of the national output is shipped back to the local supermarket. This is a lot of tonnage to ship.

One of the reasons local cattlemen ship their maturing beef far away is that the number of local slaughterhouses has fallen dramatically — down one-third in the past twenty years.[2] As these local facilities vanish, the part-time cattleman has to ship cattle much farther. The use of energy

1   Ibid.

2   New York Times "Push to eat local foods is hampered by shortage", March 28, 2010

increases, and local profitability is reduced.

Can you see how rising energy costs for fertilizer, pesticides, transportation, and packaging will impact food costs?

Some communities have taken steps to solve this problem.

One good example is found in Tacoma, Washington, where a group of local farmers banded together to form the Puget Sound Meat Producers Cooperative and bought a 45-foot-long mobile meat-processing trailer. It accommodates cattle, sheep, pigs, and goats, and is handled by six "as needed" part-time employees. The trailer travels around the region by appointment, making house calls.[1] The business plan calls for the investors to be repaid at a rate that varies from 5 to 20 percent depending on the volume of meat processed.[2]

Another good example is found in Cabarrus County, North Carolina, where a unique joint public/private venture created a slaughterhouse adjacent to a family-owned butcher shop. This enables local farmers to increase their incomes, while preserving local agriculture jobs.

Major wholesale food companies that supply supermarkets can buy the local farmers' products as well, because the new slaughterhouses produce sufficient volume, meet federal food handling standards, and are subject to daily sanitary inspection when in operation.

---

1   "Mobile Slaughterhouse helps Washington State Farmers meet demand for local foods" PBS NewsHour August 10, 2011

2   http://www.extension.org/pages/28436/puget-sound-meat-producers-cooperative

This opens up the market for the local farmers, who can sell their entire high-end product to one customer, eliminating overhead, and simultaneously offering the supermarket customer a vacuum-sealed product that earns the labels "Locally Raised," "Grass Fed," or "Organic," all of which command premium prices. Since 2008, the demand for locally raised meat in North Carolina has stimulated a 400 percent increase in the number of farmers who sell their meat locally.[1]

It may feel like a leap to link the forecasted population explosion, the rising energy consumption in India and China, and the increasing cost of putting food on our plates, but they are all quite directly connected.

As we look to the future, we can learn from communities who have shortened the distance from farm to fork, protected jobs, and created a sort of food-insurance policy for our families.

---

1   Casey McKissick, NC Choices Coordinator, 828-216-2966, as quoted from press release February 4, 2011

Prevent Misery
While Creating Jobs

Unless we do something to substantially increase food production, worldwide food availability per citizen will drop by almost half over the next thirty-five years.[1] This is because the population of the world is increasing, while production in historic farm areas is suffering the consequences of our changing climate.

The increasing drought in the west and flooding in Texas and California point to an opportunity for many states which have not yet factored this trend into their economic development plans. If we seize this opportunity, we can help prevent even more misery from being piled on top of the world's one in nine citizens who currently lack adequate food and are malnourished.[2]

The East Coast may soon lose much of the food supply that comes from California and other western and breadbasket states. Not only is it harder for California farmers to produce food in a drought or during periods of huge

---

1   Take 100% = current food availability per capita, cut production 18% = 82% available, increase population by 35% = 61%

2   The United Nations Food and Agriculture Organization estimates that about 805 million people of the 7.3 billion people in the world, or one in nine, were suffering from chronic undernourishment in 2012-2014. http://www.worldhunger.org/articles/Learn/world%20 hunger%20facts%202002.htm

gully washer rainstorms, competition for the water supply is growing. In May of 2015, California farmers (who use the majority of California's water supply)[1] saw a quarter of their normal supply shunted to California cities, which were close to running out of water.[2] The farmers were "going to have to plant 25 percent less food," they said.

When things get scarce, prices rise. Due to changes in rainfall patterns and the associated disease and insect activity, climate change puts even your morning cup of coffee at risk. In the coffee producing regions of East Africa that have been impacted by climate change, production is down 46 percent.[3] Closer to home, prices for Brazil's coffee output (one-third of the world's production) have risen 94 percent.[4]

So how does this guide us towards creating a better future? We can bring back small-scale farming.

In those parts of the United States where food production is being hit hard by climate change, the average size of farms is about 2,000 acres.[5] However, farms in heavily populated smaller eastern states, like North Carolina, average only 183 acres. These smaller farms are harder to make

1   http://www.washingtonpost.com/blogs/govbeat/wp/2015/04/03/
     agriculture-is-80-percent-of-water-use-in-california-why-arent-
     farmers-being-forced-to-cut-back/

2   http://www.nytimes.com/2015/05/22/us/california-farmers-offer-
     concession-in-drought.html

3   https://ccafs.cgiar.org/research-highlight/arabica-coffee-production-
     risk-due-changing-climate#.VWZqFly5eFI

4   http://nypost.com/2014/04/27/coffee-price-set-to-rise-as-harvests-
     decline-in-brazil/

5   http://www.nass.usda.gov/Charts_and_Maps/Farms_and_Land_
     in_Farms/fncht6.asp

profitable, but it can be done.

The challenge for a small-scale farmer is not so much the growing of the crops; it is about the cleaning, packaging, and selling in a world where middlemen want to buy an assured long-term supply in large amounts for the supermarket chains they service. Small-scale farmers need to be able to participate in large volume transactions.

It's possible. A good example of this new kind of agricultural economy is Eastern Carolina Organics, a co-op located in Durham, North Carolina. Started as a nonprofit in 2004 with a small grant, it became a member-owned private for-profit in 2005. It now coordinates the work of forty farmers and serves more than one hundred large customers like supermarkets and restaurant chains.[1]

This co-op informs customers about what is growing and when it will be harvested. Customers place their orders with the co-op, which passes them on to the appropriate member-farmers along with information regarding the needed delivery dates. The farmers transfer the product to Eastern Carolina Organics, who quality-check it, bundle it with other farmers' contributions, then package and refrigerate it until delivery.[2]

One of the ways this pooling has paid off is that planting has been tailored to local market demand. This happens in two ways: the co-op educates the large-scale buyers as to possible crops they could market, and the farmers are educated as to trends in the supermarkets that result in a more targeted supply of crops.

1   http://www.easterncarolinaorganics.com/about.php#what+we+do

2   http://www.easterncarolinaorganics.com/about.php#what+we+do

They started as a nonprofit with a grant, then became a member-owned for-profit organization, successfully carving out a niche in a free market economy. In a world where climate change is already at work, they helped increase the supply of food while others merely manipulated public dialogue. By causing a two-way flow of educational information, they created profit and jobs.

Grow Fruits and Veggies All Year-Round

As modern food processing has expanded its reach, a shrinking portion of our diet remains in its original form of fruits and vegetables. Medical professionals moan about the fact that most of us do not eat a healthy diet.

This helps explain some of the nation's rising health-care bills.

If you eat like most Americans, your grandmother would not be happy with you, "You are supposed be a role model," she would say.

Part of this unhealthy consumption pattern is due to price signals. We can buy more food for less money if we buy processed food rather than fresh fruits or vegetables. This volume is not likely to be as healthy, but it often appears to be the better choice because the larger quantity of food purchased seems cheaper.

As a nation, we need to confront obesity and other public health problems created by our eating habits; the challenge is to produce fresh foods at a cost and availability that is competitive with processed foods.

One reason that fruits and vegetables are sometimes so expensive in many parts of the country is that seasons change, and local farmers can only grow leafy greens or tomatoes outdoors for a few months each year. It is a tough business model. Traditional growers pay for the land and associated taxes for twelve months, but they only earn income from the land during a few months of the year. So they have to charge more for what they produce.

We can cheaply import food grown elsewhere, but only if two things hold true. First, it has to be inexpensive to move the produce from one climate zone to another. Second, increased amounts of fertilizer and pesticides must be added to soil to counter the depletion caused by continual use of the land. To make food affordable, these fuels and chemicals would have to remain cheap. However, for the past few years their price has continued to rise and is expected to do so indefinitely.

You can see that we might want an alternative system in place to provide us with reliable and safe food that is grown close to home, regardless of the time of year.

There is an alternative system. It is called hydroponics, and it is coming along nicely.

Imagine a piece of Styrofoam floating outdoors in a bathtub full of water. The Styrofoam has holes in it, each about as big as a quarter, which hold a spongy substance that provides a growing medium for seeds. As the seeds sprout, the roots reach down into the water. Fertilizer (which can be organic) is added to the water, and the plant grows wonderfully. Move the bathtub indoors to a greenhouse, or to a garage with skylights or artificial light, and the plants often grow better because of the lack of bugs. Fewer bugs means there is less need for chemicals, so costs go down and health goes up.

Hydroponics facilities not only grow plants off-season,

but they do so with only one-fifth the amount of water used by traditional agriculture. In addition, clever use of waste heat and natural lighting can cut otherwise expensive energy use.

One such commercial scale pioneer is Dew Drop Farm in Mocksville, North Carolina. They produce delicious tomatoes for market throughout the fall, winter, and spring when traditional methods do not work.

Restoring a healthy diet should be a matter of national urgency. With one-third of our population suffering from obesity, and another third significantly overweight, many people will end their days in declining health, or die early at great personal suffering and both personal and taxpayer expense.

One thing you can do as an individual is examine the quality of lettuce and other products at the supermarket, and compare these to their hydroponic alternatives. Then make your own decision. Another is to build a small do-it-yourself hydroponic system. If you Google "DIY hydroponics," you will find simple, inexpensive ways to get started. A quick trip to YouTube (search for *hydroponics*) will show you exactly how to do it.

With commercial expansion, hydroponics can create local, year-round employment, protect the environment, and provide a secure local food supply in troubled times. It is possible to use old or abandoned commercial or industrial property for this kind of food production if the issue of property taxes is addressed. Historically, farmland is taxed at a very low rate, but industrial property at a high rate. If local public servants were to create "indoor agriculture tax zoning," it would improve the economic climate, help ensure business survival, and also stimulate the economy and create jobs.

We can solve many of the problems facing society if we just look for good ideas already in use—and bring them home to our families.

Year-Round Harvests
Yield Local Benefits

Roughly 15 percent of all fruits and vegetables consumed in the United States are imported from outside our borders. Another two-thirds of all fruit and nut production and a quarter of all vegetables are from drought-stricken California[1] This creates a cash drain on local economies and an opportunity for bad guys to contaminate our food supply. Another very large chunk of our food supply travels thousands of miles from areas in our country that are currently struggling with drought. Shipping food from either location makes great use of oil, thus putting us doubly at risk. Weather-driven events or an oil supply interruption could not only make gasoline scarce, but it could also affect food availability—particularly healthy vegetables.

Local farmers who grow only during the traditionally warm months also have a tendency to lose their market on the back side of the growing season when relationships with customers are severed for months at a time. During times when vegetable farms are not in full production, farm crews can find themselves unemployed—and often dependent on taxpayer support.

If we could find a way to produce vegetables locally for twelve months a year, we would have the ingredients of a

---

1   www.ers.usda.gov/topics in the news

change that could make our nation's food more secure, provide more local employment, reduce taxes, increase public health, and shield food costs from rising fuel costs.

One problem hindering widespread adoption of this concept is that people have an outdated notion that vegetables cannot be grown economically year round. This is no longer true.

Eliot Coleman has been perfecting the process of raising vegetables twelve months a year using unheated greenhouses (called "cool houses") in Maine (of all places) for several decades. He has published several books on the subject.

According to Coleman, when it comes to winter gardening there are several misconceptions. For instance, it is not true that all crops need summer-like temperatures to thrive. While tomatoes may prefer warmer temperatures, some vegetables like spinach and lettuce grow exceptionally well during the cooler seasons. Another common misconception is that the hours of sunlight during the winter are too short to grow crops. Coleman teaches us that while the total hours of sunlight per day is important, equally important are the total number of hours of daylight from planting until harvest. During shorter periods of sunlight, crops do take longer to mature, but proper timing of planting across a wide range of dates can compensate for this extra growing time and result in a twelve-month harvest.

His farm uses three main principles to guide its operating philosophy: simplicity, low external inputs (including energy), and high quality outputs. By making the most effective use of this philosophy, Coleman has succeeded in creating a successful production system during a season when plants are not normally grown. The simplest technology is used to generate an economy of scale that lengthens fresh vegetable crops through winter months, while providing local twelve-month employment.

The main objective is to harvest at least three crops per year from every square foot of greenhouse—two harvests during the long Maine winter and at least one in the summer. To increase the farm's effectiveness during the unforgiving winter months, Coleman strives to select vegetables that have the greatest tolerance for cold temperatures. Then he adheres to a strict schedule for planting and harvest, and ensures vegetables are under constant cover when cold weather prevails.

Surprisingly, the vast majority of the vegetables Coleman produces during the winter are grown either in "cold houses," which use no supplemental heat, or in "cool houses," which use just a little.

The unheated greenhouses, or cold houses, produce three crops per year. Cool houses, which are designed to have slightly warmer temperatures, can accommodate six crops per year. A detailed tracking system allows the farm to determine which vegetables return the greatest economic value. Combining the field and greenhouse crops, the gross income is $80,000 per acre per year.

The findings have been documented in Coleman's books, which include *The New Organic Grower*, *Four Season Harvest,* and *The Winter Harvest Handbook.*

Producing food in this manner is dependent on labor, not machines or chemicals. As winter-producing farms become more prevalent, national security increases, local jobs are created, taxes may go down, and money that used to go out of the area to pay for food and fuel will remain in the community to create yet more jobs.

Supermarkets Are Hungry for Local Food Suppliers

A great opportunity exists to improve the health and economy of the United States.

Every major supermarket company I've spoken to tells me they have trouble obtaining reliable large shipments of locally grown produce. This is a competitive challenge for the supermarkets, because research has shown that almost 30 percent of shoppers say they would consider switching to another chain if their favorite store does not carry an adequate amount of locally produced food. Moreover, 70 percent of these shoppers say they would pay a premium of up to 10 percent for locally grown food, which would increase local farmers' incomes.[1, 2]

In order to satisfy this demand, a few industry leaders have shown the way.

Virginia's Food City grocery chain worked with the Virginia Farm Bureau and successfully grew its sales of locally grown products to about 20 percent of all vegetable sales. In addition, the effort increased local farmers' incomes from half a million dollars annually in the year

---

1   http://www.atkearney.com/paper/-/asset_publisher/dVxv4Hz2h-8bS/content/buying-into-the-local-food-movement/10192

2   http://www.kelly-products.com/Blog/tabid/104/post/The-Local-Food-Movement-Increases-Agriculture-Appreciation/Default.aspx

2000 to ten times that much in 2011.[1, 2]

Already a leader in this area, Wal-Mart in 2010 set a goal of generating 9 percent of its produce sales from locally grown produce by 2015. The company actually surpassed that goal by 2013.[3, 4]

Lowes not only buys locally produced vegetables, they emphasize their efforts by putting a face, literally, on the produce carried by posting pictures of the local farmers they buy from.

Another organization that has taken positive steps to help farmers seize this opportunity is Pilot Mountain Pride, located in the Winston-Salem area of North Carolina. They enroll local farmers via the internet and through word of mouth, offer them training opportunities, and advise them of available outlets for their product. They combine small harvests from individual farms and sell to customers who require large amounts. They also train the farmers in the national regulations around food safety, including the federal program "traceability to source."

Four issues have caused a profound change in local agriculture and have created a business opportunity.

First, food is now only one-tenth of our economy.[5]

1   http://www.youtube.com/watch?v=ntXy0tSCM88

2   http://www.knoxnews.com/news/2011/apr/03/food-city-working-suppliers-lower-prices/

3   http://www.atkearney.com/paper/-/asset_publisher/dVxv4Hz2h-8bS/content/buying-into-the-local-food-movement/10192

4   http://ag2point0.com/2013/10/28/its-a-farm-over-walmarts-admirable-ambitions-in-sustainable-agriculture/

5   http://www.plunkettresearch.com/food-beverage-grocery-market-research/industry-statistics

Almost none of the food you eat is grown near where you live; it is grown either in other countries, or 2,500 miles away from much of the population—in California. On the list of crops that we import are some real surprises. Although brussel sprouts, garlic, cucumbers, peppers, egg-plants, squash and tomatoes were all locally grown in the 1960s, almost half of these now are imported from other countries.[1]

Second, our appetites and standards have shifted. Prior to 1960, your cold weather salad would have been coleslaw, or kale and apples, or some other winter crop that stored well. Now on a winter's day you are eating a salad of lettuce, tomatoes, and peppers, all of which are almost certainly imported from parts of the world that are warm while you have your thermostat set on heat. Since field-grown summer salad contents are not produced year-round, supermarkets must import them during many months of the year.

Third, our desire for tropical fruits and vegetables like avocados, pineapples, and kiwi has grown.

Fourth, imported food gets a surprising market advantage. When food is transported between countries by air or ship, there is no tax on the fuel used, but when it is shipped from the U.S. West Coast to the East Coast, or from southern to northern states, the fuel is taxed—a lot. Consequently, it is cheaper to ship a crop like oranges from Central and South America to our East Coast than it is to ship them from California. (In 2014, the European Union introduced a

---

1   http://appliedmythology.blogspot.com/2012/01/whats-happening-with-us-fruit-and.html

proposal to change this tax structure in order to encourage energy conservation and slow down climate change, but as of this writing it is still under consideration.)[1, 2]

One way local farmers can guarantee that supermarkets have access to locally grown food twelve months a year, is by growing hydroponically in labor and technology-intensive greenhouses. The yields are *much better* than open-field farming—*twenty times greater* for cucumbers and colored bell peppers and *five times* greater for tomatoes. Why? Among other reasons, intensive greenhouses produce year-round. This would solve the supermarkets' supply variability problems, while providing the farmer with steady income.

Food production receives tax breaks and special treatment in zoning by local authorities. Since hydroponic crops can be grown in greenhouses using LED lighting right in the middle of town, or in old abandoned furniture factories and schools, this opportunity presents a challenge to how zoning and taxing authorities think. They have to set aside obsolete notions of what qualifies for agricultural treatment under these regulations. If they do not make these adjustments, it will be too expensive to raise the food locally, and we will continue to buy food grown in other nations.

The rule of thumb is that a dollar spent locally increases the local economy between $3.00 and $7.00 due to a multiplier effect, since cash left in the local economy tends to be spent there.

---

1   http://ec.europa.eu/clima/events/0036/taxation_en.pdf page 1.

2   http://www.nytimes.com/2008/04/26/business/worldbusiness/26food.html?pagewanted=all&_r=1&

Think about the local and regional economic impact if we can apply that multiplier to the 10 percent of our country's economy that is spent on food.

In order to seize this opportunity, local economic development leaders and political figures will have to demonstrate leadership. Rather than waiting for an entrepreneur to ask for a zoning waiver and special tax treatment, leadership can make those changes and advertise them. This will entice entrepreneurs to start their businesses in those areas where there is a favorable economic climate.

Link Farmers and Restaurants with Virtual Co-Ops

It is possible to create jobs, have healthier diets, and improve the local economy, all by rebirthing local agriculture on small plots of land.

Each pound of lettuce or eggs or beef shipped from Latin America or Mexico, or cross-country from California, raises our dependency on foreign oil—and buying food from far away costs us local jobs.

Some communities have figured out a new path forward that addresses all of these issues.

North Carolina's Rutherford County has one of the highest unemployment rates in the nation, and yet some 6,000 families own between five and twenty acres of land. Meanwhile, chefs in nearby Charlotte are in need of fresh produce for their restaurants.

Local leaders helped create the Farmers Fresh Market website that let Charlotte chefs and residents place orders for produce directly with these Appalachian farmers. Then, to help raise incomes, they gave local farmers the education they needed to grow more exotic items that had a higher cash value—like colorful kale and purple beans.

Two years later, Farmers Fresh Market counted ninety local farmers among its members in what amounts to a "virtual" (electronic) co-op.

Grower members of the co-op plant crops for which restaurants and schools have expressed interest. The food producers list their upcoming harvest on the website, and interested food retailers and restaurants contract online for delivery. A driver hired by the co-op makes the pickup rounds to the farms, guided by a geo-routing map for efficiency, and delivers the crops to the customers, again by geo-mapping efficient routes.

The farmers set their own prices, and the co-op takes a percentage off the top to pay for the driver and for operation of the website. The website costs about $5,000 to set up, and the buyers pay a fee of 10 percent of the sales transaction to help maintain it.

Think of the co-op as an eBay for food that connects area farmers and growers with local institutions, country clubs, and restaurants. This can cultivate a healthy agricultural economy, while also cutting down on food transportation costs and improving local diet through more readily available fresh produce.

This project has the potential to be a significant contributor to the local rural economy. Overhead is reduced by pooling the costs of transportation and marketing. Food producers are relieved from tasks they may not be skilled at, allowing them to focus their efforts and talents solely on food production. This means the final product can be priced more competitively, while still paying food producers a premium price for their product. This also increases our national security by keeping our food supply decentralized and less vulnerable to disruption either through accident or through malice.

The Farmers Fresh Market concept is being expanded into new markets, with a current focus on the upstate region of South Carolina, specifically Greenville. You can see their progress on their website, http://www.farmers-freshmarket.org. The hope is to eventually market the software and website nationally.

This is another project that becomes more possible when groups like Agriculture Extension Service join with the Chamber of Commerce and other local economic development groups, pooling their knowledge and technical infrastructure. If every community in the U.S. implemented projects like this, our country would be richer, have higher employment, cleaner air, healthier food, and lower taxes.

Aquaculture Can Cure Our Economic Ills

The population of the earth has doubled since 1970.[1] Since each of these humans needs to eat, this has led to serious overfishing of the oceans. Technical innovations such as fish finders (a type of sonar that locates schools of fish) and flash-freezing at sea, have enabled harvesting of more and more fish—too many, in fact.

No one owns the oceans or the fish that live in them. This results in unlimited harvesting in some parts of the world. The attitude of some who harvest fish is that you might as well get what you can while the getting is good, because if you don't someone else will.

Many species of fish are endangered. Many important edible fish are forecast to disappear entirely within our own lifetimes.[2] Prices will surely rise as fish grow scarcer, a reality that any homemaker can tell you is already underway.

Overfishing has exhausted breeding stocks of many favorites, such as yellowfin tuna,[3] so fishing boats are going into deeper waters to find substitutes. Do you remember a few years ago when you first saw fish like orange roughy,

---

1   http://www.census.gov/population/international/data/idb/world-popgraph.php

2   http://news.nationalgeographic.com/news/2006/11/061102-seafood-threat.html

3   http://www.minato-tsukiji.com/news_detail_2295.html

chilean sea bass, and sablefish on a menu? These fish are only found in very deep water, and their presence on a menu is symptomatic of what we are talking about here.

The deep sea is almost completely dark. Deep-sea fish grow slowly because of the limited food in these waters, and many do not reach maturity for thirty to forty years. When a mature deep-sea fish of breeding age is caught, it will take many years before another grows from fingerling to reproductive age. A fillet of orange roughy at the store is probably from a fish that is *at least fifty years old*.[1] Because of overharvesting the "mom fish," now even populations of very deep sea fish are falling sharply.

Imported fish made up around 91 percent of the seafood eaten in the United States.[2] Fish is now the second largest natural resource we import after oil.[3] Surprisingly, China is now the third ranking supplier of all food products (including seafood) to this country.[4]

One possible solution is to expand fish farming in the United States. Of all fish consumed in the U.S., roughly 40 percent is farm-raised, almost all of it abroad.[5] Global aquaculture production is valued at almost $100 billion per year, but total U.S. aquaculture production is just $1.4 billion,[6] leaving much room for our local producers to grow.

---

1   http://www.eurekalert.org/pub_releases/2007-02/osu-ldf0213C7.php

2   http://www.fishwatch.gov/farmed_seafood/outside_the_us.htm

3   http://www.noaa.gov/features/resources_0109/aquaculture.html

4   http://www.cspinet.org/foodsafety/Senatetest_Chinaim-
    ports_071807.pdf

5   http://www.nmfs.noaa.gov/fishwatch/trade_and_aquaculture.htm

6   http://www.seafoodhealthfacts.org/seafood-choices/overview-us-
    seafood-supply

One success story in North Carolina is the Taylor Fish Farm, which produces about 250,000 pounds of fish per year. They currently raise tilapia year-round, using nine antibiotic-free indoor "total culture tanks." The facility was started from scratch in 2005 and was built using only local labor. To increase profitability, Taylor sells its product through a local fish farmers' cooperative that shares the cost of marketing and other overhead expenses.[1]

Another example is the American Prawn Cooperative in Walstonburg, North Carolina. A prawn is a freshwater shrimp that grows in large outdoor ponds. This business has been expanding around 10 percent per year. It uses no chemicals and recycles most of the water it uses.

New entrepreneurs can start small, be profitable, and grow their businesses just as Bell Aquaculture of Albany, Indiana has. This company started as a backyard operation in 1994.[2] It has grown nicely, and is finishing new construction that will support the annual production of 2.2 million pounds of yellow perch (with no chemicals or antibiotics in the feed) and employ a staff of forty. Bell uses 5 percent of the water used by older fish farm designs, thus opening up possibilities for dryer parts of the country to get into this business.[3]

We know that significant business opportunities exist for modern fish farming in local markets. I have spoken to experts in the field who tell me the future is now. Indoor,

---

1   http://www.aconews.com/articles/2010/09/01/noc/news/news11.txt

2   http://www.bellaquaculture.com/about-bell-aquaculture/

3   email from Steve Summerfelt, Director, Aquaculture Systems Research, The Conservation Fund Freshwater Institute

closed system, chemical-free, low-water-use plants can be established anywhere. Housing them in old factories and other defunct buildings can lessen start-up costs.[1] Using the latest science and business techniques, and existing buildings and refrigeration facilities, new profitable local businesses and new jobs can be created, while ensuring a safe supply of locally raised food.

Cooperative Extension Services can help entrepreneurs install new local projects like these. Simply do an internet search on "USDA fish farming" to find some help.

An important part of our food supply is under threat. Fixing this using existing abandoned buildings, clever tradesmen, and knowledge of sales and marketing from your local Chamber of Commerce can bring about new jobs, food security, and improved nutrition.

Last one in the water loses.

---

1   Phone call February 22, 2010 with Dr Rick Barrows, Bozeman Fish Technology Center 406-994-9909 and Dr. Steven Summerfelt. The Conservation Fund Freshwater Institute.

Teach Someone to Fish
and You Create Jobs

According to a September 2013 federal government report, the United States imports around 91 percent of our fish and seafood,[1] a stunning increase over past decades. More than half of this fish is not wild.[2] It is raised in a fish farm. This food may not be around much longer, or it will become much more expensive, because the countries shipping them to us are growing rapidly and will need much of what they export to feed their own hungry populations.

When we import fish to eat, we also import health risks. The countries that supply us with the majority of our farm-raised seafood are not as blessed as we are with government protections that oversee food safety. They do not have strict regulation of antibiotics, growth hormones, and other pharmaceuticals commonly used abroad to help the fish survive filthy living conditions and grow faster. Once harvested, these same fish may also be introduced to unhealthy germs during the shipping phase, because unclean water systems in poor countries are used to create the ice for shipping,[3] so the fish is chilled by germ-laden water for days.

This is particularly troubling because less than 2 percent

1   http://www.fishwatch.gov/farmed_seafood/outside_the_us.htm
2   http://www.fishwatch.gov/farmed_seafood/outside_the_us.htm
3   http://www.businessweek.com/news/2012-10-11/asian-seafood-raised-on-pig-feces-approved-for-u-dot-s-dot-consumers

of all seafood being imported into the U.S. is inspected at all for filth, spoilage, or disease; less than one-tenth of one percent is tested for pharmaceuticals.[1] And here is the kicker: according to the GAO, more than half of the 2 percent of seafood inspected at our borders was unfit to eat![2] To cite just one example among many, Alabama's Department of Agriculture inspected 258 samples of fish from five Asian countries over eight years, and found that more than half contained antibiotics that are banned in U.S. fish farming due to the health risk they pose.[3]

Fish farms can be an opportunity. If fish like tilapia are raised indoors in low-density tanks under sanitary conditions, the need for hormones or antibiotics is reduced. If the fish are raised near our big cities, the time from harvest to plate is also reduced.

The beauty of this concept is that the fish can be raised in repurposed abandoned factories, shopping centers, and other similar spaces. This makes them easily accessible to food inspectors and close to the processing centers needed to turn live fish into what you find on the supermarket shelves.

Suppose your county or city were to embark on a deliberate job creation strategy based on growing sanitary seafood at the local level?

Local support can take many forms, including partnership with educational institutions. Kentucky State University (KSU) set up a business assistance center with

1   http://americannutritionassociation.org/newsletter/filthy-fish
2   http://foodsafety.news21.com/2011/imports/seafood/index.html
3   http://americannutritionassociation.org/newsletter/filthy-fish

special resources to help aquaculture business owners. Among these resources, KSU operates a mobile fish processing facility that travels around to area fish farms and helps prepare their harvests.

In nearby Calloway County, Kentucky, the local school system took the initiative and successfully applied for a grant to develop curricula aimed at high school students. Students are taught aquaculture, including how to establish this new form of raising food on small family farms.[1] This helps the students prepare for eventual studies at KSU's Aquaculture Program.[2] By so doing, local jobs and careers are developed, stemming the flow of young people away from home.

In Franklin, Maine, the Center for Cooperative Aquaculture Research (part of the University of Maine), operates a business incubator that focuses on helping existing and new fish farmers grow their businesses. The incubator also helps industry partners obtain outside funding for their research-and-development projects. Unlike other business parks, aquaculture facilities need supplies of filtered freshwater and seawater, discharge capacity, water treatment systems, and storage capacity. Business owners may utilize a few tanks for just a few days or weeks to carry out specific trials—or a whole building for multi-year projects.[3]

1   http://surfky.com/index.php/news/local/calloway/21652-calloway-
     county-school-district-receives-10000-grant-to-support-aquacul-
     ture-lesson-plan
2   http://www.ksuaquaculture.org/
3   http://umaine.edu/econdev/help-with-business-services-and-
     incubation/ Contact: Nicholas Brown—Phone: 207.422.9096 Email:
     npbrown@maine.edu.

Progress was made in both of these parts of our country because local leadership sat down and set some goals. They inventoried their assets, their culture, and their markets. They reached out to businesses and institutions that could support their goals, and they measured progress. They created a better future for their community—and so can you.

Grow Jobs
and Food-Supply Security

Consider this: the world's population doubled between 1970 and 2012 to 7 billion people. In 2020 that number will be slightly more than 7.5 billion.[1] In a few years, world agriculture will need to feed two-and-half times more mouths than it did just fifty years earlier.[2]

In order to feed all these people many changes have been made to food production. One major trend is the increased mechanization of farming, which has led to the rise of the multi-thousand-acre corporate farms in the West and the destruction of the small family farm system in the East. Another trend is the increased use of chemical weed killers and pesticides in agriculture.

When you spread weed control chemicals on a lawn or field, a few particularly tough weeds will survive and propagate. In effect, every time you spread weedkiller, you are contributing to the creation of a new breed of super weeds. Somewhere between 7 and 10 million acres of U.S. farmland are now infested with these super weeds, leading

1   http://www.census.gov/population/international/data/idb/world-popgraph.php

2   United Nations Department of Economic and Social Affairs, Population Division, Projections Section @ http://esa.un.org/unpd/wpp/index.htm

to a significant reduction in production.[1]

Some insect populations have developed immunity to chemicals that once were effective. Farmers in the United States lost 7 percent of their crops to insect pests in the 1940s. By the 1990s, that percentage had doubled to 14 percent, even though significantly more pesticides were being used.[2]

It takes years to make a new pest control chemical or weed killer—but it takes a much shorter time for a new super bug or super weed to emerge naturally. We are in an arms race that we cannot win.

Another startling fact: nearly two-thirds of our fruits and vegetables are imported.[3] As a result, employment in agriculture has dropped from one in eight jobs in 1950[4] to one in one hundred in 2014.[5] And during 2014 one in seven Americans of working age was unemployed or underemployed.[6]

It may be that we can fix all these problems at once.

The solution could be a deliberate creation of well-paying jobs through development of labor-intensive, small-scale food production in relatively chemical-free environments that are close to population centers.

Here's how it works. The food is raised in greenhouses

1   http://www.nytimes.com/2010/05/04/business/energy-
     environment/04weed.html?pagewanted=all

2   http://www.pbs.org/wgbh/evolution/library/10/1/l_101_02.html

3   http://www.nytimes.com/2013/07/27/health/fda-proposes-rules-to-
     ensure-safety-of-imported-food.html?pagewanted=all

4   http://www.agclassroom.org/gan/timeline/farmers_land.htm

5   http://www.epa.gov/agriculture/ag101/demographics.html

6   http://www.bls.gov/news.release/empsit.t15.htm

where the temperature, light, and water are carefully regulated. This extends the growing season to a full twelve months, removes risk of drought and storms, makes insect and weed control easier, and allows efficient use of nutritional enrichments. The jobs created are not minimum wage positions. I have written about Elliot Coleman, who grosses $80,000 per year, per acre, in Maine (a hard place to grow food due to its short growing season), by growing food in solar-heated greenhouses twelve months a year.[1]

These ideas and others are now being enthusiastically supported by various job-creating business incubators around the country.

At the Rutgers EcoComplex, a business incubator and sustainability research center in New Jersey, Princeton University students who wanted to be "eco-capitalists" started TerraCycle. They figured out a way to turn their college dorm's food waste into liquid organic fertilizer by feeding the food scraps to specially-selected worms. The product was such a success it was picked up for sale by Home Depot and Wal-Mart. By 2009, TerraCycle had added all-natural pet products and started selling to Brazil, Canada, and the United Kingdom. By 2011, they had one hundred employees globally.[2]

Also in New Jersey, another success is Bodi Tree Farm, which produces seasonal vegetables for restaurants in New York City. The owner came to the EcoComplex seeking education and support to enable a twelve-month growing

---

1   http://www.fourseasonfarm.com/resources/articles.html

2   http://www.terracycle.com/en-US/histories.html

season. It has been a fantastic success. Another is Olive Creek Farms, a hydroponic basil grower that within three years was able to hire the equivalent of twelve full-time employees.

If we look down the road, it is clear that it's possible to lower our nation's food risk, increase employment, and reduce the impact of chemicals on human health—all while strengthening local communities that used to be built around the family farm and could be once again.

Will you help plant the seeds of this future?

Creating

Economically

Sustainable

Local Energy

and Water Supplies

Competition Causes Conservation

When I think about what would satisfy our society's basic needs, water is at the top of my list. Not only do we need it to drink and raise food and water our lawns, it is a key ingredient in keeping our current electrical generation system working.

Making electricity requires a lot of water in order to cool the generation plants.

In the United States, power generation requires 655 billion gallons of water a year.[1] Much of that is evaporated, lowering river waters downstream.

It takes just about one gallon of water to cool the electrical generation plant needed to run one 60-watt light bulb for one hour.[2] The water used to run four such bulbs for a year will fill a family swimming pool. Multiply that by all the light bulbs, refrigerators, televisions, computers, and other electrical devices in your home, and you can see where I'm headed. In times of drought, we need to be prudent.

1 http://www.treehugger.com/clean-technology/energy-efficient-light-bulbs-save-water-too.html
2 http://allianceforwatereducation.org/why-its-urgent/6-reasons-why-you-need-to-know-about-water-right-now

The U.S. set thousands of new records for high temperatures in the past few years. During 2015, the average temperature across global land and ocean surfaces was 1.62°F (0.90°C) above the 20th century average, and the hottest in the 1880-2015 record. Almost every year is now hotter than the year before. The year 1997 which used to hold the record, has had to surrender its crown for sixteen of the past eighteen years.[1] Demand for air conditioning soared, resulting in the need for electrical generation stations to work harder. These generation stations make a lot of heat while producing electricity; they are placed on rivers so the generators can be cooled.

The same high temperatures that cause an increase in electrical demand also warm the rivers. Warmer water does not cool the electrical plant as quickly as cold water, so one of two things has to happen—either the plant uses more water for cooling, or the plant has to run at lower generating capacity. In other words, just when changing weather creates the need for more electricity, less could become available.

Some utilities are searching for creative ways to encourage customers to use less electricity. There are three major schools of thought about how to gain customer support. You can make a moral argument and appeal to a family's conscience (this does not work well except in a short-run emergency, like after a tornado). You can charge more— this works well, but it hurts poor families whose usage is already minimal. Or you can show customers how they

---

1   https://www.climate.gov/news-features/featured-images/no-surprise-2015-sets-new-global-temperature-record

rank in usage compared to other families. Surprise! This third method results in the largest behavioral change.

The magazine, *The Economist*, was inaccurate when it stated, "The only by-product of energy efficiency is wealth."[1] In some cases you get strutting rights as well.

Who says we are not a competitive nation? Our competitive nature is evident in programs used by more than sixty-five U.S. utilities that have been feeding information to their customers about how their power use stacks up against their neighbors. They do this through home energy reports and providing access to a web portal. Not only do the reports provide utility customers with information about how their energy consumption compares to their neighbors, it also provides customers with personalized ways to save energy and money.[2]

The energy information management company, Opower, runs the programs. This company takes energy usage data from a utility and combines it with public tax records—including square footage of the home, presence of swimming pools, and so forth—to uncover opportunities for energy savings. Customers receive targeted efficiency tips based on their home profile.

The results of the programs have been promising. A recent study found that customers who receive this type of information change their behavior enough to save an average of two percent on their energy bills.[3]

1   http://www.internationalrivers.org/files/attached-files/energyefficiency.pdf

2   Personal communication Ms. Carly Baker, Opower July 26 2012 via email

3   (Hunt Alcott—http://www.opower.com/uploads/library/file/1/all-

Earlier this year, Opower launched an application in partnership with Facebook and the National Resources Defense
Council intended to drive even greater savings by letting utility customers compare their energy consumption with their
Facebook friends. The application, social.opower.com, allows
utility customers to upload their usage data, and then share
and compare with other friends using the software. Currently,
seventeen utilities that partner with Opower allow their customers to automatically upload their usage data through the
application. Utility customers who do not live within one of
the seventeen service territories that use the automatic data
collection software can still participate by uploading their data
manually.

Other electronic programs allow you to turn lights and
other appliances on and off remotely. For example, if you
are on a business trip and are notified by your home ener-
gy-use monitor that your energy usage back home is too
high, you can simply touch your cell phone screen and turn
off some energy hogs. One such app is HomeMaster.[1] You
can locate information on this and other apps by searching
"home energy monitoring apps" on the internet.

Sharing energy use information with customers in this
way enables them to reduce their electric bills, head off
electrical shortages during heat waves, save precious water,
and create cleaner air—truly a win/win/win/win.

You can help your local utility have more customers put
these tools into place by presenting these opportunities at
meetings of your church or other local organizations.

---

cott_2011_jpubec_-_social_norms_and_energy_conservation.pdf)
1   http://itunes.apple.com/us/app/home-master/id423989667?m=8

Take a Fresh Look at How to Meet Your Community's Electrical Needs

Our electrical utility system in the United States works so well that headlines are made only when it fails. In many parts of the world, the headlines celebrate when the system works continuously for more than a few days!

Until recently, almost half of all electricity generated in the U.S. came from burning coal. Another quarter came from natural gas, a fifth from nuclear power, and about one-twentieth of it from hydroelectric dams.[1] As the impact of coal and natural gas on the public health and our weather have become clearer, much attention has been focused on finding better ways to keep our televisions and refrigerators humming.

In some areas of the country renewables are now making a noticeable contribution. Entrepreneurs can create electricity with wind, sun, or waste and feed it into the utility grid for use by their neighbors. These enterprises might be called non-utility generators. And they can be perceived as a threat by the existing utilities who try to either slow down their expansion or stop them entirely.

The rules that regulate utilities vary widely from state

---

1   http://www.world-nuclear.org/info/inf41.html

to state. Some states, like New Jersey,[1] encourage small non-utility generators, while others, like North Carolina, have rules and regulations that discourage renewable energy use. In addition to the variability of the state regulations, some utilities have internal policies that encourage the addition of new generation capacity by citizens, while others have policies that limit or discourage it depending on their business models.

The U.S. does not have a national electrical plan, which means we have both a mess and an opportunity.

One of the techniques used to encourage small-scale disbursed power generation is a renewable energy power purchase agreement, sometimes abbreviated as PPA. A non-utility company builds and owns the generation station (solar, wind, or geothermal) on the property of an energy user such as a school or shopping center. The company sells the power to the property owner at a fixed price under a multi-year contract that is cheaper than it would cost to buy the electricity from the local utility. There are thousands of examples.

The city of Pendleton, Oregon, used a PPA in partnership with Honeywell Building Solutions to construct a solar energy system at its sewage treatment plant. The business deal allowed taxpayers to pay less for electricity while eliminating the city's need to spend upfront capital. At the end of the twenty-year contract the city can buy the system, renew the contract under amended terms, or have

---

1   http://www.newenergychoices.org/index.php?blog_entry_id=120&
     ;page=fullstory&rd=pages&sd=df

Honeywell remove it.[1] The taxpayers saved a great deal of money, with no cash outlay.

Another technique is a feed-in tariff. This is an agreement between an electric utility and a small private power producer, such as a homeowner or a business, under which the utility will buy any cleanly produced power at a pre-set price for a fixed length of time. The largest program of this type is in Germany, but more than eighty countries[2] now use this technique, including China, which started aggressively implementing it in 2011.

The Chinese pay a premium for the clean power produced because they want to create a system of alternatives to dirty coal, which causes a lot of air pollution. Citizens everywhere who are concerned about the public health costs of coal think this is a good trade-off. Others, who focus more on the price per unit of energy only, are critical. (This has become less an issue as the cost of clean renewables has dropped in recent years; in many locations it is now cheaper than dirty power.)

These countries have other motives for creating clean alternatives, as well. By guaranteeing homeowners and businesses an income stream, the owners are encouraged to buy power generation systems from local renewable energy vendors, thus creating blue-collar jobs[3] throughout the region.

1   http://www.epa.gov/greenpower/documents/pendleton_oregon.
     pdf

2   http://www.renewableenergyworld.com/rea/news/article/2011/10/
     snapshot-of-feed-in-tariffs-around-the-world-in-2011

3   http://www.nytimes.com/cwire/2011/09/14/14climatewire-china-
     uses-feed-in-tariff-to-build-domestic-25559.html?pagewanted=all

Globally, these strategies and others like them have been proven to unleash a lot of decentralized electrical generation and entrepreneurial energy.

Some criticize the contracts because the rates paid to the owners of the renewable generation systems are higher than the prices paid to existing utilities. However, the fair comparison is between the cost of electricity generated by a new renewable energy system and the cost of a new centralized generation plant with good pollution-control systems. And, in many regions of the world and within our own country, renewables have proven to be cheaper to install and run when compared to the cost of building and running new coal or nuclear plants. All signs indicate that this will be increasingly true.

Communities often forget that they pay enormous energy bills for taxpayer-supported facilities like water and sewage plants, schools, libraries, stadiums, arenas, ball fields, and the like. If local leadership asked citizens to simply collect the utility bills and calculate the energy cost per square foot of these buildings, targets of opportunity would quickly surface. Addressing these opportunities requires investment but pays very large rates of return.

Local Investors Can Lower Taxpayer Costs and Create Jobs

One of the largest contributors to making a community poor is the purchase of energy that is created elsewhere. A dollar spent on coal or oil or natural gas leaves the neighborhood forever. It is not used to pay for local labor or local services. It is an exported dollar that hurts everyone.

A strategy that some communities have used to reduce this outflow of money is to invite private investors to invest in public and nonprofit buildings in exchange for a share of the energy savings such joint ventures can achieve.

One small but useful example of private money investing in nonprofit buildings can be found at Wellesley College, located outside Boston in Wellesley, Massachusetts. The college contracted a private investment group to replace their parking garage lights. The result: the college saved $26,536 the first year without spending a penny.[1]

The retrofit project reduced energy consumption by 57 percent, increased light levels by 32 percent, and doubled each fixture's lamp life, which in turn reduced maintenance costs. Light bills went down, and annual maintenance costs were reduced by almost $4,000. Because the private

---

1   http://www.groomenergy.com/case_study_ges_hybrid_lighting.html

investor could take advantage of tax incentives not available to the school, the actual net investment was less than $40,000, resulting in an 81 percent return on investment split between the investor and the school (which put in no money). The project was completed in two weeks, without any disruption to the parking operation of the garage.

In order to imitate these success stories, the host school, city hall, or bus system negotiates a business arrangement with a local investor who pays for new windows, air-conditioning equipment, or updated engines—all of which save money the first year, the next year, and so on. Taxpayer energy costs go down, and the investor earns a handsome rate of return from the savings. It is low risk, because if there are no savings, there is no return to the investor—and smart investors are going to make sure it will work before agreeing to fund it.

As a rule of thumb, almost any mature building can achieve a savings of 25 percent in energy costs by installing "low hanging fruit" energy conservation. This creates the opportunity for a private investor to realize a negotiated payback rate of, let's say, 15 percent for a fixed period of time, and the taxpayer might get 10 percent (with no outlay of money). Once the fixed period is over, the taxpayer receives the full 25 percent.

Additional incentives exist for private investors in the form of federal and state tax incentives, which are not available to public institutions when financing their own improvements. However, the same investment made in the same building by a private investor can qualify under some circumstances, making those investments highly profitable

for both the investor and the building owner. All of these
ventures return more than the bond market is likely to pay
for the foreseeable future.

A useful reference book on such strategies is *Climate
Capitalism*, by Hunter Lovins. In addition, the work done
by the Environmental Defense Fund Climate Corps, which
identified cost-effective investment opportunities in the
range of 46 percent reductions in energy use in public
buildings, can be found at http://www.edf.org/page.
cfm?tagID=60252.

One thing you can do is ask your elected officials how
much taxpayer money is spent on energy for public facilities, including schools. If the total amount is attention-get-
ting (and I bet it is), the officials could issue a Request for
Proposal to local private investors, giving them the opportunity to participate in a win/win project.

Many cities and towns have adopted this method
of financing energy conservation. For a very long list of
additional information, simply search for "shared savings
energy conservation" on the internet.

This kind of project does not require new technology
or have any other major barriers—except one—lack of local
leadership.

An Electrifying Idea:
Community Solar Gardens

As noted in this book's Introduction, one of my favorite statements by a corporate leader comes from Jack Welch, former CEO of General Electric, and goes something like this: "If the world outside your organization is changing faster than your organization is changing, you lose."

This is happening to many organizations that provide you with energy—and represents a huge opportunity for you and your community.

In August of 2015, the average home in the United States spent around $1,100 per year on electricity.[1] About two-thirds of that comes from very polluting and climate-changing coal and natural gas.[2] Things are heating up, as you may have noticed. Heading off trouble is going to require effort and expense to eliminate the greenhouse gas and pollution from dirty generating sources. This will make electricity from coal and gas more expensive but cut down on health-care and storm-damage expenses elsewhere.

At the same time, prices of new sources of pollution-free electricity are falling rapidly. In many parts of the country, the cost of large solar electric installations at the end of 2014 was less than five cents per kilowatt hour (kWh) and is pre-

---

1   http://www.eia.gov/tools/faqs/faq.cfm?id=97&t=3
2   http://www.eia.gov/tools/faqs/faq.cfm?id=427&t=3

dicted to continue falling rapidly.[1,2] New wind-generated electricity is down to around two cents per kWh.[3] Large utilities charge their residential customers around nine cents. People can now make their own electricity cheaper than they can buy it!

The American oil and gas trade publication, *Oil and Gas 360*, says that these falling prices resulted in two times more clean power generation being installed in 2015 than new generation from all other sources combined.[4]

Despite the good associated with clean renewable energy, there are some challenges. Wind power only works off-shore and in certain parts of the country. Solar can be hard to fit in because not all homes, schools, and other buildings get enough sun. Shade trees, tall buildings, and lot orientation can get in the way.

A positive change outside the utilities is a new form of solar ownership called a "Community Solar Garden." This is a solar electric-generation station created by many community members, each of whom own a share, the size of which varies depending on the size of their investment.

The management of the Community Solar Garden sees to it that a proportional share of the money saved by the Community Garden is applied to the specific members' electric bill at home. Investors also get their proportional share of any approved federal and state tax credits.

1   https://emp.lbl.gov/publications/utility-scale-solar-2014
2   Lawrence Berkley National Laboratory http://newscenter.lbl.gov/2015/08/12/solar-prices-fell-2015/
3   http://www.windpowermonthly.com/article/1359489/us-wind-prices-fall-66-record-low
4   http://www.oilandgas360.com/2015-coal-v-natural-gas/

Due to recent advances in battery technology, the old complaint that "the sun does not produce electricity all the time" is now obsolete. In Austin, Texas, a new 3.2 megawatt Community Solar Garden became a good role model when it included a new kind of storage battery now widely available.

Several school districts in Colorado expect to save several million dollars in utility bills by joining other citizens to create a jointly-owned Community Solar Garden project. It is located miles from the schools.[1]

Twenty-nine major firms that install large solar installations in twenty-four states are using the Community Solar Garden business model.[2] Fourteen more states are crafting legislation to make such projects easier. You can learn more about this by going to the internet and typing in "community solar platform" or "guide to community shared solar," which will lead you to a complete reference library developed by the National Renewable Energy Laboratory.

Such projects shift the role of the electric utility away from operating large generation stations toward a business model more focused on running the system of wires that carries electricity from a number of small sources to many customers.

The bottom line is that the world is heading toward smaller decentralized sources of electricity, owned by individual citizens and private investors who want to control

---

1   https://mysunshare.com/2015/07/adams-12-schools-to-benefit-from-solar-share-program/

2   http://www.greentechmedia.com/articles/read/us-community-solar-market-to-grow-fivefold-in-2015-top-500-mw-in-2020

their rising energy costs, control pollution, and keep jobs at home.

Jack Welch, to whom I introduced you earlier, would be shaking his head in disbelief at the disconnect between what is going on in some state legislatures who are resisting change while the communities they serve are seeking it.

You should be getting excited because you can take many steps that will grow your local economy.

Lower Gas Customers' Bills and Lower Climate-Change Risk

Scientists have just announced that 2015 was the warmest year on record[1] and noted an increasing number of violent storms. Signs of climate change are reported almost daily. Also noteworthy is that the language used to discuss the contribution of leaking natural gas to this emerging situation is misleading and inaccurate; it understates the problem by 1,300 percent.

Imagine your high-school daughter coming home from her first daylong tailgate party at a college football game. You detect that she has been drinking. So you ask, and she shifts her eyes away from yours and says that she had three drinks the whole time she was gone. You would be horrified—and perhaps suspicious that there was still more to the story. Further digging and tears leads you to the revelation that she was in a drinking contest and consumed three drinks in twenty minutes. Her first statement was the truth—sort of.

You imagine the risks she may have faced. Her original statement that she had three drinks in three hours was misleading because it minimized the risk of short-term impact.

Our national discussion of the role of methane (natural

---

1   http://dotearth.blogs.nytimes.com/2015/01/21/how-warmest-ever-headlines-and-debates-can-obscure-what-matters-about-climate-change/?_r=0

gas) in climate change is being conducted with the same kind of misleading statements.

Although leaked natural gas has a powerful effect on the atmosphere during its first twelve years, the media talks about its impact over one hundred years. Instead of saying we need to capture leaking gas during this twelve-year potency period when it is 150 times more dangerous than carbon dioxide from coal or oil, leaking is understated by industry as only thirty-four times worse over a one hundred-year period.

The most easily available reference tables measure the impact over one hundred years because other climate-changing gases live for thousands of years. Lost in this discussion is the recognition that if we did something about short-lived but potent gases, we would make a big dent in our problem and buy ourselves some time to attack the longer-lived gases.

Be advised that natural gas is leaking at an alarming rate in many locations around our country.

The first municipally-owned natural gas distribution system in the United States was built in Pennsylvania in 1836.[1] The gas was distributed through iron pipes. Iron pipe rusts and breaks when it gets this old, and now much of it is broken. We have enough underground natural gas pipes in our country to go to the moon and back—twice.[2]

In the summer of 2015, Professor Nathan Phillips and his teammates at Boston University equipped a car with

1   http://www.apga.org/i4a/pages/index.cfm?pageid=3329

2   http://www.fossil.energy.gov/education/energylessons/gas/gas_history.html

a new-to-market natural gas detector[1] and drove around Boston sniffing for leaks in underground natural gas pipes. They blew the minds of public officials all across the country.

The sniffing team found 3,356 natural gas leaks.[2] To learn more, you can see amazing photos by googling "images Boston natural gas." Another study of the Washington D.C pipes found 5,893 natural gas leaks.[3]

At about the same time, using another new technology, a different research team flew over natural gas production fields in Utah and found leakage rates between 6.2 percent and 11.7 percent.[4] The scale of the challenge is hard to grasp. In 1990 there were just about 270,000 working natural gas wells in the United States.[5] By 2012, that number had risen to around half a million wells across the United States, thanks to a new technology called fracking.[6]

These combined findings are stunning because for years the assumed leakage rates for the entire system, from well to kitchen stove, was estimated to be between one and three percent.[7]

    Gas output goes from wells into big pipes that span the

1   http://www.picarrosurveyor.com/
2   http://www.nytimes.com/2013/08/07/business/energy-environment/
    new-tools-pinpoint-natural-gas-leaks-maximizing-a-fuels-green-
    qualities.html
3   http://www.livescience.com/42632-washington-natural-gas-leaks.
    html
4   http://onlinelibrary.wiley.com/doi/10.1002/grl.50811/abstract
5   http://www.eia.gov/dnav/ng/hist/na1170_nus_8a.htm
6   http://www.eia.gov/dnav/ng/hist/na1170_nus_8a.htm
7   http://www.csmonitor.com/Environment/Energy-Voices/2013/0623/
    Methane-leaks-of-shale-gas-may-undermine-its-climate-benefits

country; it is then transferred to smaller pipes that enter our houses. In total, there are 2.4 million miles of leaking underground pipes in this system.[1] The federal regulatory agency, the Pipeline and Hazardous Materials Safety Administration (PHMSA), found that "seventy-two companies reported lost and unaccounted for rates of 10 percent or higher. Two hundred and seventy-five companies had a rate between 3.0 and 9.9 percent."[2] It is estimated that about one-third of all methane leakage nationally occurs in the pipes close to our homes.[3]

As a society, we face a terrible dilemma. Very smart people have discovered how to unleash vast amounts of natural gas and make a great deal of money from it. However, these recent discoveries show that the energy delivery system also allows some of it to escape at levels that not only cost customers a lot of money, but are clearly changing the climate where we live, as well. This is leading to unproductive debate, conducted mostly while individuals shout at each other—"jobs now" and "danger, danger ... climate change."

The good news is that as more violent storms and weather extremes have been observed, our society has come to realize that we need to take action. Aggressive action to stop methane leaks will result in less short-term climate change. Given the damage done over the twelve-year life span of these leaks, fixing them means their climate impact

1   http://www.aga.org/Pages/default.aspx
2   *Scientific American,* August 1, 2013, *How Much Natural Gas Leaks?*
3   http://dotearth.blogs.nytimes.com/2012/11/20/ mapping-gas-leaks-from-aging-urban-pipes/

will no longer be a problem in a few years. These efforts can have a positive impact even as the larger task of reducing CO_2 emissions is being launched.

We can also save money. The Boston sniffing team prompted Senator Ed Markey of Massachusetts to ask for the cost of the escaping natural gas. The resulting investigation revealed that the cumulative leakage just inside the cities of Massachusetts over the past ten years cost the average household around $500.[1]

Under current law, most system leakage is averaged into a customer's bill, so customers pay for leaked gas even though they did not use it. This leaves the utility with little financial incentive to fix the problem. You see, all maintenance costs money. If it only costs a little to fix a big leak, it pays to make the repair. If it costs a lot of money to fix a bunch of little leaks and customers are paying for it anyway, management is less likely to devote the resources to locate and fix the problem.[2]

We have a problem, but we also have answers. Fixing the leaks will create jobs, save customers money, and protect us from climate change. Not a bad win/win/win. All we need is public pressure on the utility operators to "step on the gas."

Student groups or others who want to take action to protect against climate change and reduce the cost to customers caused by methane leaks may be able to obtain

1   http://www.markey.senate.gov/documents/markey_lost_gas_report.pdf

2   http://www.markey.senate.gov/documents/markey_lost_gas_report.pdf

methane detectors from sources like local fire departments or gas utilities. They can even buy one from Amazon, where the prices range from a few hundred dollars for a new basic version to a quite adequate one for around a thousand dollars. What a science project that would make!

And it is likely that leak detection and repair will benefit the oldest sections of town most, lowering risk of fires and damage to those least able to afford the loss, thus improving the economic stability of the less fortunate.

Waste Can Fuel Change

Who ever thought that the route to a better United States of America might be through what we used to refer to as garbage dumps?

When measured at a dump, each U.S. citizen disposes of approximately seven pounds of garbage each day. This garbage is collected and buried at great taxpayer expense. As knowledge has increased about the dangers of accumulating garbage in dumps, an entire body of science has developed to focus on reducing the risk to our citizens. What we have now are landfills that are costly to set up and run; they require careful attention due to the chemistry that occurs when you pile lots of garbage from homes, industry, hospitals, automobile repair shops, and garden stores in one big heap. A lot of chemical "speed dating (and mating)" occurs in this dark environment. This behavior produces all sorts of unusual products while cooking away underground, and landfill operators have to monitor what is going on in order to keep the public safe.

For example, all landfills give off methane gas as old garbage decays. This gas is a notorious climate-changing substance. What is not well known is that methane lives around 12.4 years, and is "front-end loaded" in its impact on climate. As noted in a previous chapter, methane has around 150 times more impact over the first 12.4 years than the same amount of the better known threat—carbon dioxide—and has much less of an impact in later years. Because of this, any action we take that stops leakage would also slow climate change rather quickly. Would it not be wonderful if we could save money for the taxpayer while fixing this problem? It is possible for community leaders to bring this about.

There are roughly 3,000 landfills in the United States. Less than one in five is seizing a well-documented opportunity to take this mess and make something valuable out of it.[1] These 550 landfill leaders have found ways to lower taxes while using this dangerous gas safely.

There is an outstanding example of this in Newton, North Carolina, where Catawba County runs a large landfill that takes in all the trash from a more than 400 square mile area. Using the methane produced by the garbage in the landfill, the county currently runs three electrical generators that make enough electricity to power 1,400 homes.[2] When they add two new generators, they expect this number to increase to 4,300 homes—or one in every twelve homes in the county.[3] The county sells the power to the local utility, Duke Energy, at a rate that will bring the county coffers $9 million over the project's twenty-year life.[4]

These generators, like other generators around the world, make a lot of heat while making electricity. One of the distinguishing features of the Catawba landfill project is

1   http://www.epa.gov/lmop/basic-info/index.html

2   http://www.catawbacountync.gov/ue/cogen_links.asp

3   http://www.city-data.com/county/Catawba_County-NC.html

4   http://www.catawbacountync.gov/ue/cogener.asp

that this heat is captured and piped into a biofuel produc-tion and refinery station on-site. Making biofuel requires a lot of heat, which in this case is essentially free. This plant makes the biodiesel that runs the bulldozers and backhoes required by a modern landfill. In addition, research con-ducted in partnership with Appalachian State University in Boone, North Carolina, is continuing to uncover ways of producing more and cheaper biofuels in settings like this.

In other words, the managers of Catawba County have reduced taxpayer costs by taking garbage and capturing the dangerous gas that it emits and using it to make electricity. They then sell the electricity. They also use the waste heat to make the biodiesel needed to fuel the landfill fleet. This process saves the taxpayer money and helps reduce climate change.

Installing such generation and waste heat scavenging systems is expensive. Not all landfills are good candidates. The best investments are large old landfills, which have the most gas easily available. Three states—North Carolina, Texas, and California—have the most potential for landfill-to-energy projects. For example, thirty-eight of North Carolina's landfills have already been identified as good candidates, but only four of them are seizing the opportuni-ty.[1] Other states may not rank so high, but many cities and counties have unexplored potential.

Private investment is a possibility. There are many examples of the use of private capital invested by local citi-zens in situations where the local government either cannot or will not use taxpayer money for such a purpose, regard-

1   http://www.epa.gov/lmop/projects-candidates/profiles.html

less of how good an investment it may be. These investors can earn a better (and safer) rate of return by helping
solve a local problem than what they can earn by investing
in stocks these days, and they can receive tax credits for
which the local government does not qualify. These financing techniques (discussed elsewhere in this book) could be
used on landfill methane projects.

Your local Chamber of Commerce or Economic
Development Agency can work with city hall, provide the
necessary leadership, issue a Request for Proposal, and
seize the opportunity for the betterment of all.

Energy Conservation: Where Faith and Financial Communities Join Hands

In this chapter I am going to show you an area where economic public policy goals can work with the ideals of faith communities to the benefit of both.

Energy is vital for life support. Where we get it and how we use it seriously affects the design of our society. This is loaded with ethical and moral choices. All sorts of trade-offs exist, including how to reconcile the risks of supply interruption by other nations with our own national defense issues; or understanding that the installation of pollution controls might save lives while simultaneously making energy more expensive.

We have made some progress. Since 1970, energy consumption per United States citizen has dropped from one dollar of energy costs for every five dollars of Gross Domestic Product (GDP) to one out of every ten dollars in 2012. This is a real success story.[1] The myth that ever increasing amounts of energy will be required in order to grow the economy is dead.

This success has had two main drivers. First is the price

---

1   http://wilcoxen.maxwell.insightworks.com/pages/804.
     html?id=804&att=

effect. When prices go up, it drives energy consumption down. Second, government regulation has resulted in cars that get more miles to the gallon, more efficient light bulbs, and tighter building codes. However, we still have a vast opportunity to do better.

The concept that people use less of something as it becomes more expensive is easy to understand. It is much more difficult for many to understand or accept the positive role of government regulation in the area of energy use.

Decades ago a number of national incentives were put into place to encourage energy efficiency. These incentive programs allowed for-profit organizations to deduct some or all of the costs associated with investment in energy conservation from their taxes. These programs worked and have contributed greatly to the success story.

However, these incentive programs did not help the nonprofit sector. A nonprofit like a town hall, library, or hospital does not pay taxes; therefore, the tax deduction that is so motivating to for-profit companies is not available to nonprofits. This leads to expensive waste and represents a huge missed opportunity throughout the nation—in the very sector of our economy that governs, teaches, and heals us all.

Churches represent a nonprofit segment with special architectural challenges: uninsulated stained-glass windows and large spaces used for only a few hours each week (compared, for example, to a supermarket of the same size), and a small, probably part-time or volunteer, maintenance staff. Often, there is little knowledge within the congregation of the possible ways to conserve energy.

Interfaith Power & Light is a national blessing that works to help churches reduce energy expenditures. Begun in 1998 in California by an Episcopalian priest, the Rev. Sally Bingham, there are now 10,000 member congregations active in this program in forty states.[1] Some congregations start by having knowledgeable members teach other members how to do home energy audits, which generates savings in the community, if not in the church buildings themselves. Others form teams—sometimes collaborating with local schools, community colleges and universities— and do energy audits of the church property. Both of these efforts have paid off nicely.

Susannah Tuttle is the director of North Carolina's Interfaith Power and Light, headquartered in Raleigh, North Carolina. She notes that discussions among congregation members about reducing energy, pollution and climate-changing gases have the unique ability to let a broad spectrum of membership set aside their differences and work together around the notion that a dollar saved on energy is a dollar that can be redirected toward a church's mission.

Tuttle reports some wonderful success stories.

The First Presbyterian Church of Asheville, North Carolina, has a lovely old sanctuary that was constructed in the 1890s and renovated in 1951. A traditional-looking building with bell towers and stained glass windows, it also has 43-foot tall ceilings. An energy audit by congregation members identified six projects with great potential to save money.

---

1   http://www.interfaithpowerandlight.org/about/

The first project was to replace the innards of the sixty-year-old lights located up high in the sanctuary. Total cost of replacement was $4,000, but the first year's savings alone were $5,353—a rate of return of 133 percent. Multiply that by the life expectancy of the new lamps and you see that over the first five years, savings are projected to be $26,764[1]—all of which can now go towards furthering the church's mission. The other projects on their list will also pay handsome dividends.

You can bring about a positive future. Will you show these examples to members of your congregation, start a similar program, and help move our country along?

---

1   from slides furnished by Susannah Tuttle, M.Div.; Director North Carolina Interfaith Power and Light, personal telephone conversation July 10, 2013

Finger-licking Ideas
Fuel Our Future

I recall how I felt when I was a child and arrived home for family dinner, walked into the kitchen to be greeted by delicious smells of frying chicken, and was told to go wash my hands. I could not get to the table fast enough.

Little did I know that as an adult I would be writing about the role of cooking oil in energy independence and community economic resiliency.

The hotels and restaurants in the United States use three billion gallons of cooking oil per year—enough to fill tanker trucks arranged bumper-to-bumper from San Francisco to Washington, D.C., and back.[1] Most of it is used by the fast-food industry to prepare french fries, fried chicken, and so forth. This cooking oil is made from peanuts, soybeans, corn and other plants that can be grown in most areas of the country.

Over the past few years, innovators and entrepreneurs have set up a number of small businesses that make the rounds to restaurants and collect the used cooking oil. They then turn the oil into biodiesel for use in cars and trucks. The process of making biodiesel fuel is very simple (I have a neighbor who does it in his garage to fuel his own car).

---

1   http://www.epa.gov/region9/waste/biodiesel/questions.html

The biodiesel is a drop-in replacement for regular diesel, which means you do not have to alter anything in the vehicle before you can pour it into the tank. It produces almost the same miles per gallon as regular diesel but with significant advantages. First, it burns cleaner, which helps engines last longer. Second, it produces less air pollution than diesel fuel from petroleum. Third, rather than being pumped from the ground, it is made from an already existing waste product. Fourth, it costs less than diesel oil. Fifth, it contributes less to climate change. What an all-around win!

Until recently, the innovative part of this system was taking a waste product that restaurants paid to have hauled away, offering to haul it away for free (or for a small payment), and turning it into something of value. New small businesses were created, restaurants saved money, and diesel engines ran cleaner. But the challenge with this set-up was that it was often an informal arrangement that led to a lack of predictability along several steps of the process.

Bright minds began to improve the process so that it could be scaled up and become a stable and important part of our energy mix.

The Forest Foundation, created by graduates of Duke University's School of the Environment in Durham, North Carolina, developed a system that allows the biodiesel manufacturer to buy cooking oil in very large amounts, lease it to restaurants and, after it is no longer useful as a cooking tool, collect it back. The best part of the deal for the restaurants is that the lease terms are cheaper than outright purchase, and they no longer have to worry about getting rid of the used oil.[1]

Think about it: cooking oil is leased rather than purchased, and then returned when its first task is done. Then it is processed and turned into biodiesel. What we are seeing is the emergence of a new source of motor fuel that is, at this point, very small in the grand appetite our country has for oil, but exquisitely creative in the economic structure of the deal. The homegrown oils serve two purposes (cooking and motor fuel) instead of just one, and the improved economic efficiency reduces the barriers to wider use. This assists in the creation of new markets for agricultural products, while making America more energy secure. *Biodiesel Magazine* routinely publishes lists of companies working in this field. You can see this at http://www.biodieselmagazine.com/plants/map/.

Another opportunity is to combine the collection of the cooking oil with the collection of surplus prepared, but not served, food from restaurants, discussed earlier in this book. The same truck can collect both, improving the economics of both projects.

Agricultural researchers continue to lower the cost of plant-based oils at an impressive rate. Building on the infrastructure now in place to recycle cooking oils, the early signs of an economically viable, pollution-free, locally produced motor fuel point to a brighter, cleaner, and more economically stable future. You can help by sharing this information with your favorite restaurant, telling them of local entrepreneurs who are willing to take their waste oil

---

1   http://carolinabiofuels.org/

off their hands, and maybe even lease them the oil they
need for less than their current purchase costs. If you do
this, you are moving away from worrying about our future
to taking action to make it better.

Stop Flushing Money Down the Toilet

Fifteen counties in North Georgia around the Atlanta area came together to form the Metropolitan North Georgia Water Planning District. This group figured out a clever way to slow the rise in the cost of water and sewage treatment for their customers while protecting the environment.[1] This successful effort reduced water usage per capita by one-fifth with no pain to the customer at all.

First, the participants realized that only one-third of all water usage was by industry or shopping centers, etc.; the rest was by homes. This led them to examine major household uses. Nationally, about 15 to 25 percent of all water in a home is used to flush toilets.[2] They figured that if they could reduce the amount of water needed to clear toilets, they could stop flushing away money.

The group saw the value in rebate programs to encourage people who owned old wasteful toilets to replace them with modern water conserving models. In order to qualify for the rebate, the replaced toilet must use an excess of 1.6 gallons per flush. Some old toilets use as much as seven gallons per flush.[3] During this project, more than 75,000

1 http://documents.northgeorgiawater.org/2012_District_Annual_Report.pdf
2 http://www.conserveh2o.org/toilet-water-use
3 http://www.conserveh2o.org/toilet-water-use

wasteful toilets were replaced.[1]

Second, the Water Planning District (WPD) also changed the way it monitored for leaks in the freshwater pipe network.

Water districts are local entities, all wildly different in how they source their water and in the makeup of the customer base that uses it. This can make efficiency and effectiveness comparisons difficult. However, with the emergence of "big data," it is now possible to have utilities contribute information about their customer base, such as time of day and seasonal usage, and many other variables. WPD's fifty-six member utilities installed a piece of software that allows their members to benchmark themselves against each other. They can then use this data internally to detect system variances or irregularities (like leaks, theft of water, and other issues). The WPD software detected more than 12,000 leaks.[2]

These and other programs the WPD put into place have resulted in a 20 percent reduction in water use per capita.[3] This effort is worth imitating because our largely unrecognized water supply problems badly need fixing.

In 2000, the EPA surveyed our nation's water and sewer systems; they discovered that most of them were built during the 1950s. Old broken plumbing results in more than 6 billion gallons of water being lost to leakage alone each

---

1   http://documents.northgeorgiawater.org/2012_District_Annual_Report.pdf

2   http://documents.northgeorgiawater.org/2012_Implementation_Review.pdf Page 10

3   http://documents.northgeorgiawater.org/just-a-drop/0813/

year—enough to satisfy the water needs of California.

In the last five years, nearly every region of the country has experienced water shortages. At least thirty-six states are anticipating local, regional, or statewide water shortages, even under non-drought conditions.[2] When climate change is factored in, this number will rise. We are running out of time.

This is a national problem requiring local action, because 98 percent of all water infrastructure is the responsibility of state and local government agencies.[3] It will not be cheap, because there are an estimated 240,000 water main breaks a year. It will take more than $1 trillion to repair and replace systems over the next twenty-five years, according to the American Water Works Association.[4] However, for every dollar invested in water infrastructure, about $2.62 is generated in the private economy, mostly through local employment.[5]

As is often the case, these common sense good investments are not implemented until a crisis occurs. In this case, the Atlanta region suffered predictable drought both in 2007 and 2012, nearly draining Lake Lanier (it's main water source) and leaving Atlanta dry. Something had to be done.

---

1   http://www.northgeorgiawater.org/supply-conservation/water-system-leakage-assessment-reduction

2   http://www.epa.gov/WaterSense/pubs/supply.html

3   http://www.bloomberg.com/news/2013-03-19/u-s-water-infrastructure-given-d-grade-by-asce-group.html

4   http://www.awwa.org/portals/0/files/legreg/documents/buried-nolonger.pdf

5   http://www.awwa.org/legislation-regulation/issues/infrastructure-financing.aspx

Your community does not need to wait for a crisis in order to act. Water is vital to supporting life. As a country we face increasing demand, local and regional scarcity, and threats of toxic contamination. Programs like the one above can slow the rise in water and sewer bills, save precious natural resources, create jobs, and protect our ability to grow the local economy. Local civic leadership can face the opportunity knowing their efforts will be blessed by all parts of the political spectrum. It doesn't get much better than that.

A Healthy
Population
Creates a
Sustainable
Economy

Support Mothers-to-Be, Birth Healthy Children, and Lower Future Health-Care Costs

Each year in the United States, around six million women conceive.[1] (This is an uncertain number because a significant number of pregnancies end in an early miscarriage that is often not even recognized by the mother.) Another million or so pregnancies end in known miscarriages.[2] Around a million are deliberately ended by abortion.[3,4] Approximately four million children are born,[5] and a shocking and rising number of those have birth defects.

The exact number of children with birth defects is hard to nail down.[6, 7]

---

1   A calculated number derived by taking the documented number of live births, (footnote 5), adding the documented number of abortions (footnotes 2 and 3) and documented number of known miscarriages (footnote 4) to it

2   http://www.mayoclinic.com/health/pregnancy-loss-miscarriage/DS01105/METHOD=print

3   http://www.prochoice.org/about_abortion/facts/women_who.html

4   Jones RK and Kooistra, K., Abortion incidence and access to services in the United States, 2008, Perspectives on Sexual and Reproductive Health, 2011, 43(1):41-50

5   http://www.cdc.gov/nchs/fastats/births.htm

6   http://www.ncbi.nlm.nih.gov/pubmed/11745838

7   http://mchlibrary.info/alert/2013/alert011113.html

The U.S. does not have a standard definition for birth defect.[1] Some states count defects only visible at birth, like cleft palate. Some states count only those defects that were visible and corrective action was taken. For example, autism is not usually recognized until a child is in primary school. Research shows that autism has grown from one birth in every two thousand during the 1970s to one in eighty-eight in 2012.[2, 3]

Counting all the children who have late-surfacing brain defects, we now know that somewhere around one in ten of all school-age children in the U.S. are suffering from an expensive and/or life disrupting birth defect.[4] For example, the estimated lifetime health-care cost for a severely autistic child is $ 2.3 million.[5] That's for each child!

Birth defects can originate from events that occur years before boy even meets girl. Agent Orange,[6] and some agricultural chemicals,[7] can harm the father's reproductive plumbing and impact his ability to make healthy sperm. Risk increases if he is obese because this changes the way his sperm develop, and can result in an overweight son or

---

1   http://www.healthandenvironment.org/birth_defects/peer_re-viewed

2   http://www.webmd.com/brain/autism/searching-for-answers,' autism-rise

3   http://www.webmd.com/brain/autism/news/20120329/autism-rates-cdc-2012

4   http://www.pcrm.org/search/?cid=2785

5   http://www.webmd.com/brain/autism/news/20120329/autism-rates-cdc-2012

6   http://ije.oxfordjournals.org/content/35/5/1220.full

7   http://www.sciencedaily.com/releases/2010/02/100205081805.htm

daughter.[1] His daughter's weight in turn can cause harm to his grandchild because obese mothers tend to birth obese children with increased risk of birth defects.

After conception, chemicals can hurt the fetus.[2] The EPA registry of existing chemicals lists more than 84,000 chemicals currently in use,[3] almost none of them tested for fetal impact. One recent study found a total of 287 chemicals present in a baby's blood at birth.[4] In 2011, scientists in China examined birth-defect rates before and after the introduction of polluting industrial processes in a rural region; they found some rates quadrupled after "progress" arrived.[5]

A pregnant woman can harm her future child by

---

1   http://www.biomedcentral.com/1741-7015/11/29

2   http://www.emcom.ca/health/abortion.shtml: "In a study of couples living and working on Ontario farms, increased miscarriage rates were observed when certain pesticides (atrazine, glyphosate, 2,4-D, 2,4-DB, MCPA, carbaryl, thiocarbamates, and insecticides), were applied in the 3-month window of time before conception. Pesticides associated with increased risk of miscarriage when exposure occurred during the first trimester of pregnancy were atrazine, dicamba, and 2,4-D. Several studies have also reported increased risk of miscarriage in occupations associated with agriculture (e.g., gardeners, greenhouse workers, veterinarians)."

3   http://www.epa.gov/oppt/existingchemicals/pubs/tscainventory/basic.html

4   http://www.youtube.com/watch?v=0-kc3AIM_LU YouTube video of 10 Americans, report of a study by the environmental working group

5   Proceedings of the National Academy of Sciences of the United States of America, Volume 108, #31 August 2, 2011. The association of selected persistent organic pollutants in the placenta with the risk of neural tube defects

her behavior—in particular, by smoking, drinking, using drugs, or by just being obese. A pregnant woman who smokes may have a higher miscarriage rate. In addition, her offspring may have a reduction in IQ, double the chance of being mentally retarded, and an increased chance of developing childhood cancer.[1] Drinking while pregnant causes faulty hearts, problems with the structure of the mouth, nose, eyes, and head, as well as poor coordination and behavioral problems.[2] Drugs like cocaine, marijuana, and amphetamines slow fetal growth, cause heart defects, smaller brains, and poor development of the urinary tract.[3]

Obesity is a major issue. Two-thirds of Americans are overweight or obese.[4] Obese pregnant women have a significantly higher risk of miscarriage, premature births, and birthing children with defects.[5] While we cannot deny the problem, we don't need to blame Mom—her own weight issues may have been caused by her father's exposure to chemicals, as mentioned earlier.

Premature births are up 36 percent over the last twenty-five years.[6,7] One in nine children born alive now arrives prematurely, which increases the risk of cerebral palsy,

1   http://med.stanford.edu/medicalreview/smrp14-16.pdf
2   http://www.livestrong.com/article/535499-the-effects-of-drugs-and-alcohol-on-fetal-development/
3   http://www.livestrong.com/article/535499-the-effects-of-drugs-and-alcohol-on-fetal-development/
4   http://www.cdc.gov/nchs/fastats/overwt.htm
5   http://www.dailymail.co.uk/health/article-2339712/Babies-obese-mothers-higher-risk-premature-birth-illness-death.html
6   http://www.medicalnewstoday.com/articles/246413.php
7   http://www.marchofdimes.com/mission/prematurity-campaign.aspx

intellectual disabilities, hearing loss, and other issues.[1] The cost to society is enormous.

There are many ways we can help improve the health of our next generation.

Teachers can have a huge impact on young women before they conceive by stressing the value of early prenatal care. Teachers can educate young women to seek medical attention as soon as pregnancy is suspected.[2]

Moms-to-be can improve their diet and/or vitamin intake a year or so before conception. However, this is not the time for amateur hour. Health-care professionals need to evaluate the woman's health and prescribe optimal changes to diet or supplements. Vitamin A, for example, is often low in pregnant women; however, it can raise the risk of birth defects if too much is taken.[3]

There are many successful programs. One example is in Utah County, located near Salt Lake City, Utah. The health department started a pilot program aimed at helping pregnant young couples who smoke. Participants are so serious about protecting their babies that they volunteer to take ongoing "smoke-alizer" tests to confirm that they are abstaining from smoking, as well as saliva tests to determine nicotine and chewing tobacco use.[4]

---

1   http://www.cdc.gov/Features/PrematureBirth/

2   http://www.ncmedicaljournal.com/wp-content/uploads/NCMJ/may-jun-04/Meyer.pdf

3   http://www.webmd.com/vitamins-supplements/ingredientmono-964-VITAMIN%20A.aspx?activeIngredientId=964&;activeIngredientName=VITAMIN%20A

4   email correspondence with Lance D. Madigan, Public Information Officer, Utah County Health Department

At the local level, a comprehensive prenatal program aimed at high-risk groups and their partners (such as low-income workers, farm and industrial workers, and the obese) is necessary. Every dollar spent on prenatal care saves between $2.57 and $3.38 in later health-care costs to society—and a lifetime of misery for that precious life.[1]

I believe that we can, and must, invent a better future for our children. I also believe that all those Sunday School lessons about the moral dimensions of individual behavior speak to this kind of issue. A strong case can be made that taxpayers will be better off, because taking steps to reduce the number of wounded children is a lot cheaper than funding a lifetime of care. Let's invest in our next generation's future with our minds, our wallets, and our souls.

---

1   http://voicesforchildren.com/2013/03/healthy-babies-are-still-worth-the-investment-oppose-lb-518/

Use Known Science to Save Children, Reduce Taxes, and Reduce Teachers' Burdens

It takes a lot of nutrition for a pregnant woman to grow a new human being. If the right amounts of nutrition are not present in a pregnant woman's body, the baby often arrives with a brain that does not function properly.

The number of broken brains in the United States is huge and growing.

There are 62 million children between the ages of three and seventeen in the United States.[1] Somewhere around one in ten have mild to serious ADHD,[2] another one in ten have some form of dyslexia,[3,4] and another one in twenty-six have a diagnosis of other learning disabilities.[5] In addition, one in sixty-eight are affected by autism.[6]

---

1   http://www.census.gov/hhes/school/data/cps/2010/tables.html, sub-total B10:B15

2   Summary Health Statistics for U.S. Children: National Health Interview Survey 2012 http://www.cdc.gov/nchs/data/series/sr_10/sr10_258.pdf

3   http://dyslexia.yale.edu/MDAI/

4   http://www.scientificamerican.com/article/scientists-explain-rates/

5   Learning Disability Fast Facts, National Center for Learning Disabilities—I took the total population of all school aged children (62 million) and divided it by the number of children diagnosed with LD (2.4 million), yields 1 in 26

6   http://www.autismspeaks.org/what-autism/facts-about-autism

Ask any veteran teacher about the change in their students over the span of their career, and they will tell you that all these numbers are rising.

Can you see why our educational system is challenged?

The brain works by passing information from one location in the body to another, thousands of times each second. As one doctor explained it to me, "you can think about the transfer of information like tossing a ball between a pitcher and a catcher."

Problems arise when the pitcher in this analogy throws a large softball to a catcher with a hardball mitt, or a fastball when the catcher is expecting a curveball, or a wimpy pitch that does not reach the plate. Poor nutrition during pregnancy can create a poor pitch/catch process in a child's brain.

There are several reasons why the little body may have suffered poor nutrition. First, Mom's diet may have lacked enough good nutrients. Conversely, she may have eaten enough good food, but her digestive system does not work properly and so failed to absorb the nutrients. In either scenario, necessary nutrients were not available to the fetus, and the brain did not grow correctly during the pregnancy.

Many children are born prematurely. The brain goes through a growth spurt during the last three months of a nine-month pregnancy. If a child is born prematurely, that brain growth spurt has to continue after birth and must be supplemented with extra nutrition because the supply from Mom has been cut off. Unfortunately, the baby cannot make the shortage up from its normal diet during the first few months of life. Without the needed supplements the brain may not catch those fastballs and curveballs unless the child is given extra nutrition throughout its life.

By the time these children reach school age, they require more and more resources to compensate for a brain that can't catch.

A study was conducted involving approximately 12,000 pregnant women who ate various foods containing nutrients known to improve mental function. It showed that women with low intake of these important nutrients birthed children who were more likely to be in the lowest quartile of all reading scores.[1]

Here is the good news: when children are given the specific required nutritional supplements, researchers report that the "underachieving" children showed three times the expected rate of improvement in reading. They also showed improvements in spelling behavior.[2]

In a study of academic under-performers in England, 40 percent of the children given nutritional supplements showed clear improvement in learning and behavior.[3]

The surprising fact to me is that the U.S. does not act on this massive opportunity for schools to facilitate learning.

I found dozens of scientific papers outlining the size of

---

1   Lancet, February 17, 2007—Maternal seafood consumption in pregnancy and neurodevelopmental outcomes in childhood; Hibbel, Davis, Steer

2   Omega-3 DHA ad EPA for Cognition, Behavior and Mood: Clinical Findings and Structural-Functional Synergies with Cell Membrane Phospholipids, Parris M. Kidd Ph.D. P209

3   Omega-3 DHA ad EPA for Cognition, Behavior and mood: Clinical Findings and Structural-Functional Synergies with Cell Membrane Phospholipids, Parris M. Kidd Ph.D. P209

the problem and the effectiveness and low cost of the solution. Schools regularly do hearing and vision testing, but I could not find one example of a school system that systematically ensures that their students are tested for this very common barrier to learning.

Adults have an opportunity to model the behavior we want from our children. We expect our children to be conscientious about doing their homework; we can do our own science homework and change our school systems to incorporate what we have learned.

If we do this, we will improve the lives of millions of children and families forever, and we will reduce the cost to the taxpayer for health care and special education. Truly a win/win for our society.

You can start by checking out the footnotes in this chapter, or go to Google Scholar (a special website for scientific researchers) and search on "nutrition deficiency," "autism," "ADHD," "learning disability," and "dyslexia."

Invisible Threats to Moms Have High Cost

Common sense tells us, and scientists have confirmed, that if the average person can sense an immediate threat to their family such as lightning from an oncoming violent storm, the person will do something to avoid the danger. However, without those visible signals, there will be little incentive to change. The worst kind of threat to warn people about is one that is invisible.

A real world example is one that is threatening pregnant women. It is from an unseen pollutant in the water that gets into the fish we eat. If the pregnant mom consumes enough contaminated fish, she will damage the brain of her unborn child. I am talking here about mercury, introduced into the environment from burning coal to make electricity. This practice is the major contributor to the fact that one out of every six women of childbearing age has unsafe levels of mercury in her blood; this results in as many as one in ten[1] children being at serious risk for brain damage.[2,3] How

1   http://www.cdc.gov/nchs/fastats/births.htm

2   http://www.cdc.gov/nchs/fastats/births.htm

3   There are around 4 million live births per year and " between 300,000 and 600,000 children are estimated to be at serious risk for severe neurological and developmental impairment from mercury exposure each year" . From Mahaffey KR, U.S. Environmental Protection Agency, 2004.

much harder it is to catch a mother's attention when she cannot actually see the evidence of those unsafe levels. (For more information on this problem in your neighborhood, Google "Mercury + Fish + Pregnancy+ your state name" — but sit down first.)

Long ago medical scientists were able to teach us that smoking and drinking while pregnant were not good for the baby. You may also remember the painful lessons learned from birth defects caused by some medicine taken while pregnant (think Thalidomide). Now our knowledge of how pollution also contributes to harming children's development has expanded.

California researchers conducted a study of 30 million births over a six-year period. They found a strong association between higher rates of birth defects among women who conceived in the spring and high levels of agricultural chemicals and garden pesticides in water during those same planting months. The study showed a link between the springtime conception and higher rates of birth defects for half of the twenty-two categories of birth defects, including spina bifida, cleft lip and cleft palate, clubfoot, and Down syndrome.[1]

It is also clear that other issues do not surface until a child enters school; these result from exposure to pesticides or other chemicals, as well as to other forms of pollution during pregnancy. As science continues to recognize more kinds of injury to children that are not visible at birth, we have come to see that our system for reporting birth defects

---

1   http://health.usnews.com/health-news/family-health/womens-health/articles/2009/03/31/study-links-pesticides-to-birth-defects

is probably not showing the full picture.

Similarly, there is a link between the quality of our drinking water and the quality of our health.

Consider this: in North Carolina, just about half of all homes get their drinking water from private wells that are not tested regularly. Even when they are tested to the limits of the law, much is undiscovered. Why? While the U.S. government regulates the levels of bacteria or virus in drinking water, it has no rules for pharmaceuticals and other compounds, apart from the herbicide atrazine.[1]

There are things you can do to help unborn children everywhere. In your own home or office, you can use less electricity by changing five light bulbs from the old kind to those with an ENERGY STAR rating. Referring to statements made by the Environmental Protection Agency, "if every household in the U.S. just changed five lightbulbs, we could prevent the pollution equivalent to nearly 10 million cars."[2] Keeping your car tires properly inflated significantly reduces air pollution, because soft tires require the car engine to work harder. And you can be cautious about your family's drinking water by buying an inexpensive water filter that removes heavy metal pollutants. You can get one for around $35.00 at the hardware store.

So here is today's exam question: have you or your community done anything to reduce the impact of pollution on your children? If not, what are you going to do about it?

---

1   http://www.ewg.org/sites/tapwater/national/unregcontams.php

2   _http//www.epa.gov/climatechange/wycd/home.html last updated April 14, 2011

Polluted Schools Damage Brains

Since the passage of the Clean Air Act in 1970, the United States has become much healthier. According to the *New England Journal of Medicine*, our average lifespan increased by almost three years between 1978 and 2001, and as much as 4.8 months of that increase can be attributed to cleaner air.[1] For people living in more polluted areas, like Pittsburgh and Buffalo, clean air increased life expectancy by ten months.[2] Every dollar spent on that effort returned more than thirty dollars in savings in medical and other costs.[3]

Some would argue we should now turn our attention to other pressing national issues, like our education system. Critics complain that schools are not doing their job. Educators respond that the student body of today is nothing like those the parents remember from their days in school. And they are right.

Ironically, a key but unacknowledged part of the education debate is air quality.

The number of students with brain damage from air pollution is significant.[4]

---

1   New England Journal of Medicine, January 2009
2   New England Journal of Medicine, January 2009
3   Benefits and Costs of the Clean Air Act 1970 http://www.epa.gov/air/sect812/design.html ; Second Prospective Study — 1990 to 2020 http://www.epa.gov/air/sect812/prospective2.html
4   "Air Pollution Around Schools Is Linked To Poorer Student Health And Academic Performance," - Health Affairs, May 2011

According to the National Center for Health Statistics, over the past decade the number of children diagnosed with developmental disabilities increased by 1.8 million.[1] Between 10 to 15 percent of all babies born in the U.S. now have some kind of neurobehavioral developmental disorder.

Researchers have identified two major pieces of the puzzle. First, doctors at the Saban Research Institute at Los Angeles Children's Hospital found that the children of mothers exposed to air pollution from fossil fuels and industrial chemicals during pregnancy are five times more likely to have attention deficit hyperactivity disorder (ADHD) and other learning issues.[2]

The second piece of the puzzle is that despite the overall progress made in cleaning up our nation's air, a major contributor to brain damage is air pollution in and around schools.

Children are not little adults. As they grow, they go through a series of "windows of vulnerability" that increase the likelihood of pollution sneaking through. They take in twice the amount of air per pound of weight than an adult does, and their brains represent a larger portion of their total body weight.[3] Students attending schools located

1   Bloom B, Cohen RA, Freeman G. Summary health statistics for U.S. children: National Health Interview Survey, 2009. National Center for Health Statistics. Vital Health Stat 10(247). 2010

2   Perera FP, Chang HW, Tang D, Roen EL, Herbstman J, Margolis A, Huang TJ, Miller RL, Wang S, Rauh V. 2014. Early-life exposure to polycyclic aromatic hydrocarbons and ADHD behavior problems. PLoS One 9(11):e111670

3   Health Affairs (Millwood). 2011 May;30 (5):842-50. Epub 2011 May 4. Children's vulnerability to toxic chemicals: a challenge and opportunity to strengthen health and environmental policy

within several hundred feet of busy highways have significantly higher damage to their brains than those located farther from pollution.[1]

University of Michigan scientists found that in addition to any birth defects they might have, children who lived in or attended school in areas with high pollution during their first five years of life also developed problems with concentration, reasoning, judgment, and problem-solving.[2] They also had lower IQs.[3]

As concerned parents there are some things that you can do. You can set up an "Idle Free Zone" — a designated area where, due to its proximity to a school, you must shut off your car's engine. A kit of instructions, tools, and training videos is available from www.momscleanairforce.org. A study done by Cincinnati Children's Hospital found such programs to be very effective in creating a safer environment for children.[4]

---

1   Environ Health. 2007; 6: 23. Near-highway pollutants in motor vehicle exhaust: A review of epidemiologic evidence of cardiac and pulmonary health risks Doug Brugge, John L Durant, Christine Rioux

2   Journal of American Medical Society, March 25, 2015, — "Prenatal exposure of common air pollution linked to cognitive, behavioral impairment."

3   http://news.umt.edu/2015/02/021015alzh.php UM Study Finds Air Pollution Affects Short-Term Memory, IQ and Brain Metabolic Ratios Feb. 11, 2015

4   Environmental Science Processes and Impacts, September 2013

In addition, you can work with school administrators to install modern indoor air filters that can reduce pollution by one-half or more.[1] Lawrence Berkley Labs, managed by the University of California at Berkeley, found that every dollar spent on cleaning the indoor air in a school saved $33 previously lost through poor attendance of both students and staff.[2]

School systems can also install air filters on their school buses to protect riders. The University of California at Los Angeles developed an on-board school bus filter system that reduced air pollution by 88 percent. When riding on one of these buses, a child inhales air that is as clean as the air on the beach at Santa Monica.[3] Washington State monitored children on 188 school buses from 2005 to 2009. The children who rode buses with pollution-reducing equipment had a six-percent reduction in absences — in addition to a lower risk of brain damage.[4]

And talk about adding insult to injury — is it fair to blame teachers for not doing their jobs effectively when their students, whose minds have been damaged, are not able to pass standardized tests?

---

1   Air Pollution for Nearby Traffic and Children's Health, California Air Resources Board, 2004

2   Association of Classroom Ventilation with reduced illness absence — Indoor Environmental Group, Lawrence Berkeley National Laboratory, May 2013

3   UCLA Media Contact Ms. Kim Irwin, 310-794-2262

4   "Adopting clean fuels and technologies on school buses: Pollution and health impacts on children," April 21, 2015 University of Michigan News

Reduce Air Pollution
with Roundabouts

Using roundabouts instead of traffic lights or stop signs has been documented to save as much as 20 and 30 percent of the fuel consumed at intersections, with corresponding declines in solid and particulate pollutants.[1]

A study in Vermont considered the hypothetical state-wide installation of roundabouts in place of signals at just one hundred busy intersections. They estimated a decrease in total annual motor fuel use of approximately one to two percent as compared to 1997 annual statewide gasoline consumption attributable directly to the roundabout. They also estimated a similar one to two percent improvement in land-use density.[2] In other words, installing a rather modest number of roundabouts throughout the United States, in a distribution similar to the Vermont study, would directly save twice as much gasoline as drilling for offshore oil would produce under the model proposed during the

---

1   Varhelyi A (2002) The effects of small roundabouts on emissions. Transportation Research Part D 7. pp. 65-71 (Elsevier Science, Oxford, UK).

2   Canadian Transportation Research Forum, Vancouver, May, 2001. Modern Roundabouts, Global Warming, and Emissions Reductions: Status of Research, and Opportunities for North America

2008 election.[1,2] It would also reduce air pollution instead of increasing it.

The city of Carmel, Indiana, also found that when roundabouts replaced traditional intersections, accidents with injury were reduced by 78 percent.

Two decades of intersection control modeling, software development, and research have established that roundabouts rather than traffic signals at busy intersections save substantially on fuel. By extension, they reduce pollution emissions and Green House Gases (GHG)—also demonstrated through analysis of empirical data, as well as through modeling reported from existing U.S. roundabouts and those under development. This knowledge base is so well accepted that it is included as a modeling assumption in highway planning computer models[3] and is a recognized (although grossly underused) design tool.

---

1   http://www.celsias.com/article/drill-baby-drill-how-media-has-influenced-americas/

2   http://www.eia.doe.gov/oiaf/aeo/pdf/trend_4.pdf

3   Highway Capacity Manual compatible software, aaSIDRA

Replace Vehicle Fuel Caps, Reduce Air Pollution, Save $500 a Year

Everyone knows that your car has a gas cap. You may not know that many of these leak—in some cases around 30 gallons a year! According to the U.S. Car Care Council, 17 percent of vehicle gas caps are either damaged or missing, allowing 147 million gallons of gasoline to vaporize every year.

Gas caps can leak regardless of the age of a vehicle (although they are more likely to leak if a vehicle is more than three years old). Every leaking gas cap equals approximately 200 pounds of evaporative emissions per year—equal to 0.1 tons of Volatile Organic Compounds (VOC), a particularly awful form of pollution.

Taxpayer-supported fleets (school buses, police cars, etc.) have a great opportunity to increase miles per gallon (MPG) by reducing evaporative losses.

Between 2007 and 2009, Mecklenburg County Air Quality (MCAQ) in Mecklenburg County, North Carolina, provided gas cap testing units to rotate among volunteer North Carolina inspection stations. More than 18,000 vehicles were tested. More than 800 gas caps failed the test and were replaced. This prevented more than seventy-eight tons of evaporative emissions from being released annually into the atmosphere and saved more than 23,000 gallons of fuel. When the faulty gas caps were replaced, the owners of the cars saved around $500 each year.

MCAQ also conducts gas-cap testing at businesses, special events, and other community venues in the Charlotte ozone non-attainment region, a part of the country that has been declared unhealthy due to the levels of ozone. Counties in the Charlotte region include the North Carolina counties of Mecklenburg, Gaston, Lincoln, Iredell, Rowan, Cabarrus, Union, and the adjacent South Carolina county of York. If a vehicle's gas cap fails the test, a new one is provided free of charge. The program is funded by an $89,000 grant from the North Carolina Department of Transportation, and MCAQ staff and volunteers administer the gas-cap checks.

In other words, one $89,000 grant saved 800 drivers an average of $500 per year, for a total of $400,000 per year for each year of the remaining life of those cars. For more information, contact: Alan Giles, Mecklenburg County Air Quality.

New-Breed First Responders
Help Solve
U.S. Health-Care Crisis

Some of the costliest health care delivered in the United States starts with a call to 911. This triggers an expensive ambulance run, which usually results in an expensive emergency room visit. After recovery from the specific crisis the patient goes home, only to start the billing cycle over again with another call to 911 when a similar crisis re-emerges. These patients might be called "frequent riders."

One role model worthy of learning from in this arena is MedStar, a government-run ambulance system serving fifteen towns in the Dallas/Ft. Worth, Texas area.[1] They have figured out how to reduce the number of calls to 911, how to respond to them more quickly, how to have a more highly trained ambulance crew, and how to improve patient care—while at the same time reducing total health-care costs.

Here are a few of the techniques they use.

First, MedStar matched its fleet to the need by examining how often calls for help came in and from where. On review, they discovered that the majority of the calls came

---

1   Page 2, City of Ft. Worth Ambulance Assessment, the Polaris Group 273 North Dogwood Trail, Southern Shores NC 27949 — 252.441.8844

during two peak times of day, but historic staffing schedules had the same number of trained people standing by
in ambulance garages all day long. By changing to twelve-
hour, overlapping shifts, they were able to have 50 percent
more crews standing by during peak call times.[1] This had
two results: faster response times, and a much lower payroll since they no longer had to pay for excess staff during
the quiet times.

In addition, depending on the time of day, ambulances
that used to wait at a garage or fire station were moved to
locations that historically generated the bulk of 911 calls.
Think of it as defensive football: if you know a pass is
coming, you deploy your defense against it. Again, shorter
response times.

To deal with frequent riders, MedStar did an analysis
of who called for the ambulance and for what purpose.
They found that twenty-one callers resulted in nearly 1,000
ambulance calls in one year.[2] These callers generated $1.1
million in ambulance charges and nearly $2.5 million in
emergency room charges.[3] Reducing the number of such
calls would save time and money for the company—and
taxes that covered uninsured riders. In addition, if they
played their cards right, they could improve the health of
the frequent riders.

Armed with this list, MedStar assigned a paramedic
on light duty to make what amounted to house calls in

1   Matt Zavadsky Associate Director Field Operations—MedStar by
     phone 817-632-0522

2   Ibid.

3   Ibid.

order to check up on patients who had suffered on-the-job injuries. These house calls uncovered many circumstances that would have resulted in further calls for help if not addressed. Because of this kind of intervention, the use of the ambulance service by these callers declined by 51 percent.[1]

Another technique that helped was to review with the frequent riders the cost of the ambulance and hospital. Many often had no idea of the cost, and some changed their behavior when educated.

MedStar did further research on other assumptions— and found some surprises. Research demonstrated that "running cold" (no lights or sirens) instead of screaming down the road did not increase the time from the first call to the arrival at the hospital. However, it did enable the EMT (emergency medical technician) crew to tend to the patient more effectively (putting in needles, and so forth) without the patient or the EMT being thrown from side to side when brakes were applied or abrupt turns occurred. The patient actually arrived in better shape without the use of sirens.[2]

The ambulance service also noted that they had a high percentage of calls to large gatherings where mature guests suffered heart attacks. Even if people with medical training were among the guests, they were unable to assist the patients because the event hall did not keep a defibrillator on hand. Through the MedStar website, party planners can now request the loan of a defibrillator to have on hand at

1   Ibid.

2   http://fortworthtexas.gov/citynews/default.aspx?id=84124

the party,[1] thus raising a heart attack victim's chances of survival.

In addition, MedStar made training more efficient. Now when the crews are on call but not busy, they can log into trainings via electronic distance learning. During times with no emergencies, the crews are in school.

MedStar began in Fort Worth and grew as other area cities recognized the value of joining a regional system. The system now includes 55 ambulances and 325 employees. They have more than 200 fully-licensed and highly trained EMTs and Paramedics. Thanks to the "training while wait-ing" plan, a large number of those now hold advanced certifications.

---

1   http://www.medstar911.org/medstar-aed-loan-program

A Sustainable

Economy

Lowers Crime

As of January 2016, the United States had a population of 319 million.[1] While the U.S. has only 5 percent of the world's population, it has nearly 25 percent of its prisoners—about 2.2 million people.[2] We have the highest percentage of citizens behind bars of any nation in the world. China, with four times more people, is a distant second.[3] In addition, the number of people on probation or parole brings the total population of the U.S. corrections system to more than 6,851,000, or one in every thirty-six adults.[4]

1   United States Census Bureau website

2   http://www.apa.org/monitor/2014/10/incarceration.aspx

3   http://www.pewtrusts.org/~/media/legacy/uploadedfiles/pcs_assets/2010/collateralcosts1pdf.pdf

4   http://www.bjs.gov/index.cfm?ty=pbdetail&iid=5519

> The prison population is largely the result
> of tougher mandatory state and federal
> sentencing that has been imposed since
> the mid-1980s. Minorities have been hit
> particularly hard.

One in every ten black males in their thirties are in prison or jail on any given day.[1]

Generally speaking, a jail holds inmates from two days up to one year. Prisons are for people convicted of crimes that carry a sentence of one year or more. The most notable difference is that prison inmates have been tried and convicted of crimes, while those in jail may be awaiting trial. A prison is under the jurisdiction of either federal or state government, while a jail holds people accused under federal, state, county, and/or city laws.

Drug offenders make up 19.5 percent of all jail inmates in the United States, roughly 470,000 people. In the federal system, drug offenders account for well over half of the 200,000 prisoners, for a combined federal and state total of around 600,000 people out of the 2.3 million people who were behind bars as of January 2009.[2]

About one half of all inmates have committed violent crimes. [3] This group has the highest rate of repeat offenses, most of which are caused by lack of impulse control—a

1   http://www.sentencingproject.org/template/page.cfm?id=122

2   http://stopthedrugwar.org/chronicle/564/US_jail_prison_population_all_time_high_drug_offenders

3   http://www.ojp.usdoj.gov/bjs/glance/tables/corrtyptab.htm

key symptom of a brain that has not developed in a normal way, often as a result of pollution and stress surrounding the mother during pregnancy, and unhealthy environments while the young brain is still developing. As you read in earlier chapters, good science now exists that shows us how to prevent this, and in some cases correct some of this damage and improve behavior.

A surprising fact is that in the states with the highest rates of incarceration, many of those behind bars are there not for crimes of violence, or drugs, but for failure to pay child support.[1] Many of these people cannot find work, either because of prior arrests, or due to a poor local economy.

If one believes that children adopt the behavior of their role model, by the same logic, if a child's role model spends time behind bars, the child might also follow in that direction. This is indeed the case, as many children of prisoners are prone to becoming prisoners as well.

It costs taxpayers approximately $30,000 annually to keep each prisoner behind bars in a government funded institution, compared to $25,000 to enroll an individual in a state-funded four-year college where they can earn a degree—with tuition, room, and board covered.

Within state governments, operating the jail and prisons costs around one out of every fifteen tax dollars—and this is climbing.[2]

Now consider this: in the U.S., unlike other countries,

---

1 http://www.nytimes.com/2015/04/20/us/skip-child-support-go-to-jail-lose-job-repeat.html?_r=0

2 Ibid., page 2

roughly 40 percent of the people who spend time behind bars return there within three years.[1] Ex-cons typically are unemployable; their options for making a living are largely illegal. Their disregard for socially beneficial rules of behavior may still exist, and now they have the added burden of having limited ways to make an income.

Remember: all prisoners except those with life sentences get out of jail and return to their neighborhoods. They are often unemployable, and in many cases are surrounded by the same circumstances that led them into trouble in the first place. If we face those facts squarely, we must ask, "What can we do to lower the recidivism rate of prisoners, get them off public support, and convert them from a drain on social capital to a contributor?"

Many successful programs reduce imprisonment and avoid the repeated offenses against society that result in jail time.

For example, a variety of surveys have found that between 40 and 60 percent of all people behind bars have at least one learning disability.[2] These challenged citizens are more likely to learn healthier ways to live if the underlying problem is addressed. Many suffer from vitamin deficiencies that are the result of poor absorption, which could be remedied with vitamin shots. Once supplement-

---

1   http://townhall.com/news/us/2011/04/13/pew_study_prison_recidi-vism_rates_remain_high/page/full/

2   http://www.ncbi.nlm.nih.gov/pubmed/10876375

ed in this way, the inmates settle down and are able to learn basic skills, and often more complex ones.

Our law enforcement and corrections problems can be summarized as stemming from:

- a decline in intact two-parent households
- a high rate of neurological birth defects and learning disabilities due in part to "food deserts" that increase consumption of unhealthy food and drink and help create obesity
- pollution-contaminated housing and schools which lead to reduced IQ and impaired impulse control
- children imitating their imprisoned role model parents
- the difficulty in finding a job once convicted (which leads to further crime in pursuit of income)

Our society has created a pool of people dependent on social safety nets, with no resources and training to wean them off.

Unless we can figure out how to break this cycle, the future will contain more of the same, posing a huge road-block to fostering the growth of a healthy society.

Make Your Community Safer, Salvage Lives, and Lower Taxes Via Inmate Education

As noted earlier, the United States has the highest rate of imprisonment of any of the advanced societies in the world. One out of every one hundred of our adult citizens is behind bars at any one time.[1] The numbers are even more startling when you add in the number of offenders on parole or probation, which results in one in every thirty-six adults under some form of correctional supervision at any one time.[2]

The cost is enormous. The average cost of maintaining a person behind bars is around $30,000 per year in the United States.[3] To make matters worse, roughly 40 percent of people who spend time behind bars in the U.S. return there within three years[4]—often because their status as excons makes them unemployable and the available options for making a living are largely illegal. This too is peculiar to the U.S.

---

1   New York Times, 2/28/2008, reporting on, and quoting from, the Pew Center Public Safety Performance Project

2   Pew Trust press release "1 in 31 U.S. Adults are Behind Bars, on Parole, or Probation." 03/02/2009, contact Jessica Riordan 215-575-4886

3   Ibid., page 2

4   http://townhall.com/news/us/2011/04/13/pew_study_prison_recidivism_rates_remain_high/page/full/

There is some good news. One of the emerging strategies is to train incarcerated people in a trade or skill that they can practice as a self-employed entrepreneur or within a very small (often family-owned) business, where they are well known and will have watchful family eyes on them.

In Florida, one successful program teaches inmates how to keep bees. A national expert in hive management trained nineteen inmates. During their six-week training program, they produced more than 600 pounds of honey for use in the prison kitchen. This is not a make-work program. It is run in conjunction with Florida's Department of Agriculture and Consumer Services, which is concerned about the impact of a declining native bee population on Florida's citrus crop. Industry officials are interested in talking to graduating beekeepers, especially those who are at the end of their sentence, about employment. The waiting list among prisoners to get into the program is long and growing.

In North Carolina, the Community Culinary School of Charlotte (CCSC) trains an average of fifty former prisoners, recovering drug addicts, and other hard-core unemployables each year to be chefs and cooks. Its success is astonishing. Since June of 1998, CCSC has graduated more than 640 people and has an 85 percent placement rate. The job-retention rate after six months is 86 percent. Graduates are placed in local restaurants, country clubs, retirement centers, and in institutional food establishments.

They also serve during their training program, preparing 5,000 meals for other social service programs each week!

Compared to the cost of keeping a person behind bars,

the cost of such training is quite small, and the fiscal conservatives among us will delight in the rate of financial return.

Our nation is facing many challenges—including little-discussed problems like declining bee populations to pollinate our crops and prisoners who commit repeat offenses. With courage and honesty, we can select the right inmates, spread a little honey around, make our society safer, and lower our taxes.

Children of Prisoners Can Be Saved

According to the Department of Justice, many of those behind bars have children. Parents who have spent time behind bars serve as role models to one in every twenty-eight children in America today.[1] Hmmm. What kind of future are we headed for?

Research from as far back as the year 2000 tells us that unless something is done, about 70 percent of the children whose parents are involved in the correctional system will end up involved themselves.[2] Think about that for a moment. Approximately three of every four children whose parents have been imprisoned for committing a crime have a high likelihood of becoming criminals themselves—unless something is done to prevent it.

In 2000, three people—John DiIulio, Professor of Political Science at the University of Pennsylvania; Judy Vredenburgh, President and CEO of Big Brothers Big Sisters of America; and Rev. Dr. Wilson Goode Sr., former Mayor of Philadelphia—met to discuss the dilemma of how to help children with a parent in prison. Working together, they started recruiting mentors for the children of inmates from forty-two church congregations in Philadelphia, and

1   Pew Research Center's Economic Mobility Project, September 28, 2010
2   U.S. Senate Report 106-404 September 8, 2000

the Amachi program was created.[1]

There are now more than 250 versions of the Amachi program working in various areas of the U.S., drawing thousands of adult volunteers from many churches and other organizations. [2]

One good example is the program located in Texas. It started in 2006, and places children of prisoners in a special Big Brother program so that they may have a second, more positive, role model. In some cases, the "little brother" or "little sister" is paired with a firefighter, and during visits to the fire station, becomes "adopted" by the whole fire crew.[3] The program includes children ages six to fourteen, who stay an average of twenty-three months in the program with their big brother or big sister.

The results are astounding.

Ordinarily, when students in Texas act up badly in school, they are removed and sent to a special room or school so as not to disturb the other students. With the Amachi program in place, there has been a documented 88 percent reduction among the children who participate in the program having to be removed from their regular classroom. And less than one in fifty of the Amachi children have entered the criminal justice system themselves— again, less than the national average. Better yet, 96 percent of all the Amachi children earn promotion to the next grade. This is well above the promotion rate of children

1   "Big Brother Big Sisters Amachi—Positivity affecting children im-
     pacted by parental incarceration 2010

2   Amachi: "People of Faith Mentoring Children of Promise", www.
     aecf.org/MajorInitiatives

3   Amachi website http://www.amachi-texas.org/index.php

who do not have a parent behind bars.[1]

Due to its success at salvaging lives and lowering tax-payer costs, the Amachi Program has spawned imitations in almost all fifty states. The program has attracted the support of churches, politicians (President Bush was an enthusiastic supporter), and many institutions. The program received federal taxpayer support between 2003 and 2011, until Congress cut the funding.

Since the early 1980s, the number of our citizens behind bars has quadrupled,[2] and we have only taken baby steps to reduce the impact this will have on our society. Fortunately, Amachi and similar programs are showing us that we can invent a better and safer society.

---

1   All statistics on the success of the Amachi program were gathered during a personal phone call with Ms. Olivia Eudaly, State Executive Director of Amachi Texas, held February 15, 2012

2   Incarceration rate of inmates under state and federal jurisdiction per 100,000 population 1925-2008, Bureau of Justice Statistics.

Citizens Help Solve Crimes

This is a crime story with an unexpected ending, where the bad guys can behave like good guys if we give them the right tools. The result is that the police can spend their time catching more bad guys.

Reported crime in the United States has been steadily dropping for many years. Murders, burglary, and car theft dropped by more than half between 1980 and 2009. Reports of rape also dropped 22 percent.[1] This reduction is good news.

The bad news is that the rate of solved crimes is also falling. What the cops call the "clearance rate" (an arrest has been made, the case has been turned over for prosecution, or the criminal is dead) has dropped from around 90 percent in the 1960s to below 65 percent in recent years. Police fail to make arrests in more than one third of all homicides. And in recent years, there has been a decline in arrests made for crimes against property.[2]

It used to be that we had a neighbor against neighbor crime pattern, where the background, historic animosity, and network of multi-generational families offered law enforcement access to information and many ways to investigate. Now we have more of a gang against gang pattern,

1   Table 306, Crimes and crime rates by type of offense:1980 to 2009, US Census Bureau Statistical Abstract of the US, 2012

2   2004_UCR_crime_clearance.jpg

where crimes are often committed by strangers against other strangers, and those who help the police may suffer retaliation.

We need a system that increases the chances that criminals will be caught the first time they commit a crime. Since many offenders commit multiple crimes, catching them the first time may reduce the likelihood that the behavior will be repeated.

One voluntary citizen initiative in place to help police solve more crimes is called Crime Stoppers. Begun in 1975, the program has two key ingredients. The first is that it pays a reward. The second is that it keeps the identity of the crime reporter a secret.

Traditionally, Crime Stoppers posts its phone numbers around town. When someone has information about a crime, they call either a local or national phone number (the national number is 1-800-222-TIPS), make a report, and are issued an identification number. If the information is accurate and helps lead to a conviction, the tipsters get back in touch with Crime Stoppers, identify themselves by the identification number, and receive their reward. There are now more than 1,200 local chapters.[1]

Since its founding, Crime Stoppers tipsters have contributed information that has led to more than 600,000 arrests. They have collected a million dollars in reward money, and have helped confiscate drugs valued at more than $3,000,000.[2] In many cases, the rewards are not accepted; the tipsters tell Crime Stoppers to keep the money and

---

1   http://www.augustadps.org/crimestop.html

2   http://www.crimestopusa.com/

use it to get more bad guys off the street.

In Collier County, Florida, after rumors of expanding drug use in the high school began to spread, special efforts were made to let students know of the local Crime Stoppers phone number. In a two-week period eighteen arrests were made, half of which came from tips phoned in by students.[1]

Now here is a clever idea about how to make this good system work even better. Some Crime Stoppers groups are working with local jail and prison systems to make it easier and safer for inmates to offer tips.

In Tallahassee Florida, concerned citizens and law enforcement produced 100,000 decks of special playing cards. The cards were printed with regular playing card symbols of hearts, clubs, diamonds, and spades on one side and details of unsolved crimes on the other, along with the Crime Stoppers contact information. The cards were made available to inmates, and tipsters behind bars furnished information that solved two murders as a result.[2]

In Tulsa, Oklahoma, the sheriff's office processes 32,000 inmates a year, with an average daily population of around 1,700. Many of the 32,000 are in jail for just a day or so until bail is posted. Crime Stoppers tip line phone numbers are included in the handbook issued to all new inmates, as well as publicized elsewhere in the jail.[3] Based on phone records, Tulsa corrections officials know that the Crime Stoppers phone number is being called from the phones reserved for

1   http://www.floridacrimestoppers.com/

2   http://www.fdle.state.fl.us/Content/Office-of-Statewide-Intelli-
      gence/Menu/Cold-Case-Playing-Cards-Home.aspx

3   E-mail communication Ms. Shannon Clark, Public Information Of-
      ficer, Tulsa County Sheriff's office

inmates' use. They also have indications that when a short-term inmate hears gossip or bragging about a crime while in jail, they often call in the tip when they return home or can access a public phone.[1]

What we have here is a volunteer program that is working impressively in 1,200 locations; however, it could be even more effective if its marketing were expanded aggressively into the locations where the criminals are being held. We can make our society safer if we just give the inmates the tools.

---

1   E-mail communication Ms. Shannon Clark, Public Information Officer, Tulsa County Sheriff's office

Feeding
the Poor
Reduces
Taxpayer
Health-Care Costs

Feed Your Soul—and the Poor

We have a messy public-policy debate underway about how communities and various levels of government should "love thy neighbor as thyself" through ensuring access to food. Some communities have taken interesting steps to improve the efficiency of the food delivery systems as a way of expressing that love.

According to the U.S. Census Bureau, one in seven (46 million) of all U.S. citizens now fall below the official poverty level[1]—and this rate has been rising for the past decade.[2] If you are a couple with two children, the assumption in the definition of poverty allocates only 79 cents per individual meal to feed your family.[3]

The growth in the number of people struggling to put food on the table has resulted in an increased demand on various charities. This has collided with a dramatic national reduction in donations, down 8 percent since 2007.[4]

---

1   http://www.epi.org/publication/ib339-us-poverty-higher-safety-net-weaker/

2   http://stateofworkingamerica.org/chart/swa-poverty-figure-7m-poverty-rate-actual/

3   http://budgeting.thenest.com/typical-percentages-household-budgets-3299.html

4   "Total giving in 2012 was 8.2% below giving in 2007, before the charitable sector felt the effects of the recession. If the pace of growth in charitable giving stays constant in the coming years, giving will not rebound to pre-recession levels until 2018." http://

We have a growing needy population—and less to offer them. You can see a very sobering map of the problem by Googling "map the meal gap."

In response, a movement has begun that coordinates the production of food grown by local churches, volunteers, schools and others in this spirit of "love thy neighbor." Resourceful communities can now create systems that deliver predictable harvests in large quantities for use by charities. Rather than planting small quantities of beans, corn, or tomatoes, all of which ripen at different times, the church (or other organization) is instead asked to deliver a specific harvest, say twenty bushels of corn on a particular week in July. This arrangement dictates the kind of corn to be planted and the planting time. Caring for the garden becomes easier, and the food pantry knows when to expect the crop and can plan accordingly.[1]

As the supply of locally grown healthy food has expanded, food pantries have discovered something interesting. One third of adults in this country don't know how to cook fresh food.[2]

Cooking does not mean warming up leftover pizza or defrosting a Weight Watchers meal. Cooking is the ability to take a bunch of just-picked vegetables, or a piece of uncooked meat, and turn them into something the family

---

www.charitynavigator.org/index.cfm?bay=content.view&cpid=42#. UgKDcKwueSo

1   http://www.theoptimisticfuturist.org/index.php/component/content/article/25-publishedarticles/201-community-efforts-relieve-food-insecurity.html

2   http://www.huffingtonpost.com/2011/09/09/cooking-survey_n_955600.html

would want to sit down and eat. The adults of yesteryear were simply better trained to cook than today's adults.

Here is the situation. An increasing number of people need food on the table, but there is less money to run the food pantry programs. At the same time, local efforts to grow fresh food for the needy have expanded, but a declining number of people know how to cook. This is a mismatch that needs local action to solve.

The historic role of the food pantry or soup kitchen needs to expand from simply handing out food to also training people in food preparation.

A good example of an innovative program in food preparation and preservation is run by Triad Community Kitchen in Winston-Salem, North Carolina. It started a job training program to teach future food handlers how to prepare ready-to-heat meals.[1] In partnership with Forsyth Technical Community College, the program provides training in food handling regulations as well as cooking skills.[2] Working under the close supervision of certified chefs and college faculty, the trainees practice their emerging skills by preparing food for distribution to the hungry.

North Carolina's Second Harvest Food Bank Program now integrates both the trained workers and the food processed during training at Triad Community Kitchen into their overall effort. In 2012 this program contributed to the successful distribution of 21.3 million pounds of donated, purchased, and prepared foods through a network of more than 400 partner food-assistance programs in North

1   http://www.hungernwnc.org/about-us/index.html
2   http://www.hungernwnc.org/how-we-work/tck.html

Carolina. It has served more than 18 million meals to the poor.[1]

Elsewhere in North Carolina, people are being trained to cook through a creative program called Hunters for the Hungry. The program allows local hunters to donate deer and other wild game to be converted to stew meat or burgers. Last year, Hunters for the Hungry donated more than twenty tons of ground venison to the needy.[2]

Our country is full of success stories about how local leadership figured out a way to help their community, often while simultaneously lowering taxes, increasing the number of people helped, and increasing community and individual self-reliance. The more I learn, the more I am convinced that we don't lack ideas or role models. We just need more local leadership willing to take these good ideas and put them into place.

Chew on that for a moment. How do you fit into that picture?

---

1   http://www.hungernwnc.org/about-us/index.html
2   http://nchuntersforthehungry.org/About_Us.html

Community Efforts Relieve Food Insecurity

In my home state of North Carolina, about one child in six lives in a household where it is not clear where the next healthy meal is coming from. This is called "food insecurity," a term used by the United States Department of Agriculture to describe people "... without reliable access to sufficient quantity of affordable, nutritious food."[1] Nationally, food insecurity impacts 48 million of our citizens, including 15 million children.[2]

Many of these children take part in school lunch programs; summers without school and these lunch programs mean increased hunger.

Those in leadership positions at local social services agencies tell me these numbers are not only real but perhaps even on the low side. They point out that donations to charities dropped in recent years by more than 8 percent from previous years—so there are more people who need help while there is less money being donated to the helping agencies that feed people.

Some communities have figured out how to increase

---

1   http://www.ers.usda.gov/topics/food-nutrition-assistance/food-security-in-the-us/measurement.aspx#insecurity

2   http://www.feedingamerica.org/hunger-in-america/impact-of-hunger/hunger-and-poverty/hunger-and-poverty-fact-sheet.html?referrer=https://www.google.com/

the supply of food for needy families during times when donations of money have declined.

Harvest Now, based in Westport, Connecticut, was started by Brooks Sumberg, a recently retired salesman (and former Peace Corps volunteer in his youth). Sumberg learned that donations to food kitchens serving the poor had significantly declined when the economy in his part of Connecticut collapsed several years ago. Hungry people were being turned away from soup kitchens and food banks due to lack of food.

Working from his home, he began to call area churches to see if he could persuade them to start a congregation garden and donate the harvest to those feeding the poor. It worked.

Started in 2009 with planning for the 2010 growing season, the program coordinated eight area churches as they established gardens. The first year they produced 2,100 pounds of food, enough to put fresh vegetables on 8,400 dinner plates. Three years later the program had grown to forty-eight churches and one prison; by harvest season 2012, the program was on track to produce more than 12,000 pounds of food — in a part of the country with a short growing season.

The program has learned some valuable lessons in its brief life. High spoilage rates of produce such as lettuce led the group to focus on foods that are easier to store, like squash and potatoes that do not require refrigeration. Challenges included the need for reliable sources of water during the growing season and transportation during the harvest. Later on, the need to recruit new volunteers arose as some of the early participants moved on to other areas of interest.

To help a community get started there are websites that contain training materials, planting schedules, lists of resources and coaches, and a host of other materials. One example is Gardening Matters (www.GardeningMatters. org). Another is the American Community Gardening Association (www.communitygarden.org). I discovered that well-organized efforts can get seeds donated by public-spirited companies like Baker Creek Seeds, Botanical Interests, Ferry Morse, and Seed Savers Exchange.

Now comes the "think big" part.

It is possible to increase the value of such efforts by developing a master plan that asks the right questions in order to get the answers that will shape the choice of crops planted.

First, identify the recipients of the harvests. Second, find out when the harvests would be most helpful; some charitable organizations I spoke to said that they may get drowned in tomatoes for a month or so, and then nothing — not because tomatoes could not be grown but because no one asked the gardeners to plant early or late season varieties. Third, schedule pickups and deliveries effectively; it is a heartbreak for volunteers when lovingly-tended beans or peppers spoil because not enough thought was given to this step. The transportation process can also be simplified if gardeners focus on growing fewer varieties, but larger quantities of each type. This prevents the pickup system from having to visit dozens of gardens, collecting only a few cucumbers from each. And this enables the gardeners to become expert on a few kinds of vegetables rather than having to learn about dozens.

Taking care of our neighbors can involve both the heart and the head. Creation of a coordinated plan can vastly multiply the loving work that is willingly done. We can create a better future for our families, our neighbors, and our country by imitating successful programs already in place. Will you help?

Rescue Hungry People

Each day in the United States one in seven households either does not have enough to eat or does not know where next week's food is going to come from[1]—and this number is steadily increasing as chronic unemployment rises. This contributes to personal misbehavior and rising crime rates, and weakens the fabric of our society.

Knowing that, consider this: about a quarter of all of the food available for consumption in U.S. supermarkets and restaurants is thrown away uneaten.[2] Restaurants in some states have been shown to toss out more than half the food they prepare—not scraps, but unserved meals.[3]

Much of this food is wasted because restaurants and other potential donors fear they will be sued if someone eats the donated food and claims they got sick from eating it. Rather than run that risk, they throw the perfectly good food away.

They don't need to—a federal law exists that shields them from lawsuits. Many years ago such laws differed from state to state, and national companies felt at risk when being asked to make food donations. They asked Congress to make it easier to donate.

---

1 http://www.feedingamerica.org/hunger-in-america/impact-of-hunger/hunger-and-poverty/hunger-and-poverty-fact-sheet.html
2 https://www.nrdc.org/food/files/wasted-food-ip.pdf
3 2006 study by California Integrated Waste Management Board.

The Bill Emerson Act was passed nationally in 1996 with the sponsorship of President Clinton and then Rep. Newt Gingrich. It provides a uniform standard of liability protection across state lines.[1, 2] This allows large national firms like Target and Kroger to adhere to one set of standards. Despite this law, many local supermarkets and restaurants still do not donate food.

It seems that the folks who knew about the law upon its passing in 1996 have moved up, or on, and their younger replacements often do not know what is allowed. The company vice president approaching retirement age may know it is safe to donate excess food, but the current shift manager at the restaurant may not know.

Some organizations and communities have been successfully grabbing this opportunity for a long time. We can learn from them.

In addition to uncooked foods from supermarkets, there are two major sources of safe, previously prepared food that could be donated. One is from places that serve large crowds for special events: banquet halls, country clubs, and conference centers. The other is from restaurants that serve food all day, every day. Both groups could donate food if a few simple steps are taken.

Think about the role of food in celebrations—it is surrounded by good emotion. People eat at wedding banquets, birthday parties, and business ceremonies. Awards are

---

1   https://www.gpo.gov/fdsys/pkg/PLAW-104publ210/pdf/PLAW-104publ210.pdf

2   http://media.law.uark.edu/arklawnotes/2013/08/08/the-legal-guide-to-the-bill-emerson-good-samaritan-food-donation-act/

given, songs are sung, and toasts are made. Participants applaud and give standing ovations. All this happens in rooms laden with plates of food. When the room clears and the flowers are collected, when trophies are carefully packed into the car and last photos taken, a national tragedy begins to unfold, out of sight of the now departed guests. The carefully prepared leftover food is thrown away.

Not far from these venues of celebration are places where poor people, lacking the means to obtain their next meal, line up to get something—anything—to hold body and soul together.

The first step involves a change of process during the planning of the event. Since the people hosting the party are paying for the food, it really isn't up to the club or hotel to give it away. The host of the party, or the event planner, should bring up the question of donating leftovers to charity. If the desire to make the gift exists, a simple donation form could be offered to make the gesture official, and the staff could then proceed to arrange for the food to be picked up.

The second simple step involves scheduling. A charity will often get a call late in the evening saying something like this: "If you get here before we close you can have meals for fifty." This leaves the charity worker with the challenging task of rounding up a vehicle (possibly containing refrigeration) and a driver at the last minute, often after bedtime. A better way is for the meeting host or food service staff to contact the receiving organization a day or so before the scheduled event and inform them of the possibility of a food donation.

Restaurants are another potential source of food. They purchase large amounts to cook on a regular basis, some of which goes unused if demand for certain menu items is small. With expanded recruiting of donor restaurants, the existing collection route could be expanded, providing larger amounts of useful food.

One of the keys to increasing the amount of salvaged food donated is to have refrigerated trucks collect the donation. Another is to have the crews of those trucks hold certificates of safe food handling. When donors see a quality operation like that, donations rise. They don't worry that their act of generosity might result in the distribution of spoiled food.

In California, more than 90,000 stores are licensed to serve food and beverages. Thanks to the efforts of Food Donation Connection, a donation coordination service, 940 of them (including Pizza Hut, KFC and Chipotle Mexican Grill restaurants) donate surplus food. You can see more about these efforts at their website, Food to Donate.[1] Think about the good that could be done if the other 89,060 stores got on board!

In western North Carolina, the MANNA Food Bank collects and distributes food to 255 charities that feed those in need. They maintain a fleet of refrigerated vehicles with full-time drivers, a drive-in freezer and a drive-in cooler, and they even collect from gardeners.[2] You can learn more about them at www.mannafoodbank.org.

What can you do? Try reaching out to the companies

1   http://www.foodtodonate.org/

2   www.mannafoodbank.org

that are likely to have surplus foods and encourage them to expand their programs. Or show this chapter to your local grocery, restaurant or country club.

Throwing away good food creates disposal costs for the organization throwing it away, costs taxpayer money to expand expensive landfills, and increases the strain on churches and other caregiving organizations that often have to buy food to feed the people they serve.

Diverting food from landfills will also slow climate change, because decaying food in landfills is one of our nation's major sources of leaking methane, a climate changing gas eighty-six times worse over a twenty-year period than CO_2.[1]

To top it all off, a corporate donation actually increases the profit margins of donors, because they get a tax deduction for the charitable contribution. What an all-around win!

Your local church group, high school clubs, or public servants can get this process underway by creating a list of establishments that could be potential donors but have not yet signed on, as well as a list of the area organizations that feed the hungry, like soup kitchens, rescue shelters, and some churches. Once you have the lists, including phone numbers and managers, publish them side by side in the local paper.

Then publish the lists again two weeks later, noting any signs of cooperation. Keep it up until there are no names left on either list. Then have a party.

---

1   http://www.climatechange2013.org/images/uploads/WGIAR5_
     WGI-12Doc2b_FinalDraft_All.pdf

Thoughts
to Cling
to as You
Bring About
Change

You Are Fighting on Behalf
of Innocent Victims

In almost every area of civic life where change is need-ed, you are fighting on behalf of innocent victims. You can draw some measure of comfort because a review of history shows that over time such efforts have often succeeded in having laws, regulations, or new innovation created to re-duce the damage done.

The phrase, "mad as a hatter," is falling into disuse. I suspect many of the children wandering around with deaf-ness-inducing ear buds dangling think it refers to a charac-ter in Alice in Wonderland. They are wrong.

Back in the eighteenth century, top hats were made out of felt, which was pressed and shaped using a rinse that contained mercury. During the process, mercury entered the hat maker's body little by little, causing what we would today call an occupation-related illness. Eventually, the worker went mad.

While "mad as a hatter" and the underlying origin have faded, it has been replaced in modern society by other ways in which people are damaged while working. Back in the late 1960s, modern medicine told us that many people were in harm's way because of dangerous chemicals and prac-tices in the workplace, and in 1970 a law was passed to pro-tect workers. It is called the Occupational Safety and Health

Act (OSHA).[1] Since the creation of OSHA, worker deaths have been reduced 65 percent, this during a period when the workforce has doubled.[2] OSHA costs each citizen about one-and-a-half cents each month.[3]

With all of this progress, the full story is still not being told. Left uncounted are the many illnesses caused today by chemicals that were not even known in 1970. These illnesses can damage the employee's family more than they damage the employee.

First, we hurt innocent, and often unborn, babies. Second, because the jobs where these chemicals are used tend to employ workers who are paid a low seasonal wage, we are creating a damaged permanent underclass that finds it hard to get or hold another job. Good examples of this kind of social cost are in the fields of agriculture and lawn care. Think about your recent wave "hello" to the familiar face of the neighbors' lawn-care guy. Chances are his children have a higher rate of birth defects than other families.

In Denmark, a study collected information on 24,000 live births. The study examined 17,000 normal children and more than 7,000 children with birth defects. More than 6,000 of the cases with birth defects had cryptorchidism (absence of or undescended testis at birth of a male child) and more than 1,000 cases of hydrospadius (the urinary opening is not in the correct location on the head of the penis).

1   http://www2.epa.gov/laws-regulations/summary-occupational-safety-and-health-act

2   https://www.osha.gov/oshstats/commonstats.html

3   The budget of OSHA is $535 million in 2013 according to the footnote above. There are 306 million Americans. Divide 535 by 306, and again by 12 = .015

The researchers found much higher rates of birth defects among children of users of agricultural chemicals.

Here in the United States, evidence has been accumulating for decades. Here is just one summary drawn from a National Resources Defense Council report summarizing peer reviewed science:[1]

> Mothers living in counties of high
> agricultural productivity or with high
> pesticide use were found to be at greater
> risk of giving birth to children with limb
> reduction defects than mothers living in
> areas of low agricultural productivity and
> low pesticide use.[2] A study of pregnant
> women in Iowa and Michigan found an
> association between maternal exposure to
> multiple pesticides and an increased risk
> for cleft palate in offspring.[3] A new study in
> Minnesota found a significantly increased
> rate of birth defects in the offspring of
> private pesticide applicators.[4]

1   http://www.nrdc.org/health/kids/ocar/chap5.asp

2   Schwartz, D.A., and J.P. LoGerfo, "Congenital Limb Reduction Defects in the Agricultural Setting," Am. J. Pub. Health, vol. 78, no. 6, June 1988, pp. 654-658.

3   Gordon, J.E. and C.M. Shy, "Agricultural Chemical Use and Congenital Cleft Lip and/or Palate," Archives of Environmental Health, vol. 36, no. 5, 1981, pp. 213-220

4   Garry, V. et al., "Pesticide Appliers, Biocides, and Birth Defects in Rural Minnesota," Environmental Health Perspectives, vol. 104, number 4, April 1996, pp. 394-399

Not all of the birth defects are visible. An October 2014 study by researchers at the University of California at Davis found that children of women who lived within a one-mile proximity to pesticide spraying during their second trimester had a 50 to 640 percent greater frequency of autism than children of women who did not. The study also found that children of women who lived within a one-mile proximity to pesticide spraying during their third trimester had a 10 to 260 percent greater frequency of autism than children of women who did not. The study stated, "The majority of pesticides sold in the United States are neurotoxic."

As a result of our public policy, we've created a new class of people who require extraordinary social support because of the damage done to them while in the womb. Over time, these victims may not have the mental capacity to work at modern jobs, or they are damaged in ways that require extensive social support, and some percentage engage in behaviors that result in expensive prison time.

If we gaze through the lens of a world where morality guides the way we construct society, we will remember the commandments that say we will not kill or steal—even if it is cheaper. Yet that is exactly what poorly tested and regulated chemicals are doing. As a community leader, you can ask to see what chemicals are being used in your community, in what amounts per year, and then quickly look up the risks these may cause. Risks may be entirely absent. Or they may be many and great.

Cities like Toledo, Ohio, distribute tips for their citizens on how to reduce the use of lawn care chemicals.[1] You

---

1   http://www1.toronto.ca/wps/portal/

can make sure your local political jurisdictions do not use chemicals around playgrounds, and you can help our local politicians imitate successful programs elsewhere.

You Can Make a Difference

The United States has begun to turn the tide on how we deal with child abuse. I am not saying the problem is solved, but progress—compared to where we started decades ago—is being made. The lessons here inform many other challenges our society faces.

The term *child abuse* covers much ground, from lack of food and hygiene, to emotional abuse, to battery, and to sexual abuse. Using that broad definition, it appears that out of the roughly 75 million Americans under the age of 17,[1] more than one million of them are victims of child abuse each year.[2] More than half of the abused are reported to suffer from neglect. They may not be physically attacked, but they are not fed or supported in ways that their young bodies and minds require. Of the remaining group, about 300,000 suffer physical abuse, about 150,000 suffer emotional abuse, and around 135,000 suffer sexual abuse.[3] It's hard to believe these numbers represent progress, but they do.

In 1873, a church volunteer doing a home visit found a nine-year-old girl chained to a bed, malnourished, and beaten. The volunteer's first efforts to rescue the child failed, because the law and custom of the day made such behavior

1   http://www.childstats.gov/americaschildren/tables/pop1.asp

2   http://pediatrics.about.com/od/childabuse/a/05_abuse_stats.htm

3   http://pediatrics.about.com/od/childabuse/a/05_abuse_stats.htm

within a household a private matter. Local officials ignored the reports, and when investigation was finally begun, the community leaders failed to follow up. In desperation, the church worker turned to the American Society for the Prevention of Cruelty to Animals for help, because animals were protected under a better set of laws than children were. ASPCA sued the officials, arguing that humans were animals too. The resulting publicity successfully rescued the child.[1,2]

Starting from this foundation of outrage against physical and emotional abuse, science helped build the case. With more widespread use of x-ray technology in the 1950s, doctors began to see examples of years of abuse documented in untreated and badly healed fractured bones of children who previously had no witnesses to their situations. In 1962, the *Journal of The American Medical Association* summed up this horror in an article that called for diagnosis and treatment of child abuse as a medical condition.[3]

As knowledge of both emotional and physical abuse grew, discussion of sexual abuse of children, heretofore a taboo subject, became more acceptable.

There was resistance. Some labeled these efforts as intrusion into the arena of the family and/or an unwarranted expansion of government. Some called the emerging evidence poor science. State and local laws became an uneven patchwork quilt, resulting in people getting away with bad

1   http://www.child-abuse-effects.com/history.html
2   http://family.findlaw.com/child-abuse/child-abuse-background-
     and-history.html
3   http://jama.jamanetwork.com/article.aspx?volume=181&;issue=1&p
     age=17

behavior in one locale that would be unacceptable some-where else—not much different than today's legal climate in the area of public health and the environment.

The first comprehensive federal law protecting children from abuse did not pass until 1974. The Child Abuse Preven-tion and Treatment Act, or CAPTA, required states to create systems to capture and investigate reports of child abuse.[1] As a result, a large number of children were removed from bad circumstances.

There were problems. In the beginning there were no standardized training programs for how to investigate a sus-pected case of child abuse.[2] Imagine this situation in other professions: ambulance crews who have never been trained in CPR, or police officers who have never been trained in hos-tage negotiations. Yet this is exactly the situation that existed for many years with regard to child abuse. Finally, in 1985 the National Child Protection Training Center, which developed undergraduate and graduate curricula in investigation and prevention of child abuse, was started at Winona State Uni-versity in Minnesota. Since its establishment, the center has trained more than 100,000 child-protection professionals.[3]

We have come a long way from the days when animals were given more protection than children. While the jour-ney is incomplete, much can be learned by studying how change was brought about.

1   A brief history of Child Welfare System published by Pew Trusts 2004

2   Victor I. Vieth, "Unto the Third Generation: A Call to End Child Abuse in the United States Within 120 Years," Journal of Aggres-sion, Maltreatment & Trauma

3   http://www.gundersenhealth.org/ncptc/about-us

This history teaches us that concerned citizens can shine attention on problems and bring about changes in customs and laws for the betterment of all. We also see that, as science and technology give citizens clearer insight into problems, your ability to bring about change increases.

Don't Confuse *Price* with *Cost*

One type of resistance you may encounter when you propose change will be the issue of what people will label as *cost*. This word is frequently misused; if you address the issue early in your advocacy, you will keep your project on track.

In a capitalistic economy such as ours, the notion of a *price* signal is a key, often unstated, assumption. So let's make sure you understand the difference between *price* and *cost*.

If your neighbor had a beef cow that routinely broke the fence and ate your hay, your neighbor would get wealthier at your expense.

Because the guy who owned the cow did not have to pay for some of the cow's food, the *price* he charges for the butchered beef could be artificially low. You subsidized him—you provided part of the true *cost* of production and you received no compensation. The *price* and the *cost* of the beef were not the same—but they should have been. Your subsidy of your neighbor disrupted free market economics because the "price signal" was not accurate.

There are two kinds of subsidies that cause price and cost to take different paths.

The first is outright government subsidy that is practiced by many governments around the world.

Our own government has a long history of taxpayer subsidies to emerging industries as a way of helping them get on their feet. Recipients include the railroad industry in the 1800s, the oil and gas industry in the early 1900s, the coal industry in the 1930s, and the nuclear power industry in the 1950s. The current hot political debate about picking winners and losers has been going on for almost 200 years.

To illustrate the impact of how subsidy impacts public policy, it is interesting to look at the history of taxpayer subsidy for energy suppliers. Serious academic and financial industry analysis shows that the highest subsidies occur during the first fifteen years of a new energy industry.

For example, when comparing renewable energy (solar and wind) to nuclear power, coal, and oil, the studies found that nuclear received eight times more subsidy than renewables; oil received five times more; and the natural gas industry also received five times more.[1] These subsidies to nuclear, coal, and oil continue in some form today, and they distort social choices by sending the wrong price signal. They mislead the marketplace. To counter this, advocates of new forms of energy cry foul and ask for similar subsidies, while the historic beneficiaries argue against the very blessing they received in their industries' early years.

The second form of subsidy I like to call the "cowpoop subsidy." Imagine that the same cow belonging to your neighbor—the one who ate your hay—also wandered into your living room and left you a present. You would have to pay to have the mess cleaned up. Again, because your

---

1   http://www.dblinvestors.com/documents/What-Would-Jefferson-
     Do-Final-Version.pdf

neighbor moved some of the clean-up costs off his books and onto yours, his selling *price* to the consumer can go down while your *costs* go up. Your pain was his gain.

Many organizations are interested in behaving like your neighbor with the cow. They would like to get subsidies and leave a mess behind for others to pay to have cleaned up.

The cowpoop subsidy can be shown in all areas of our economy. Here are some examples from the coal industry: West Virginia University researchers found that citizens living in coal mining towns have a one-third greater incidence of high blood pressure, a two-thirds higher risk for developing chronic obstructive pulmonary disease (COPD), and a more than two-thirds higher risk of developing kidney disease. In areas near mountaintop coal removal mines, the rate of birth defects was 235 per 10,000 live births compared to 144 per 10,000 live births in non-mining areas, according to a separate study done in 2011 by Washington State University. This is the *cost* paid by these victims so that the *price* the rest of us pay for coal-fired electricity is kept artificially low.

When this coal is burned to make electricity near your home, this kind of cost becomes yours as well. Health-care costs for communities located near coal-fired electrical generating plants, totalling in excess of $4 billion annually, are two to five times greater than the costs for communities located farther away from coal plants.

Take all of those health costs, add to them the cost of taxpayer subsidies, and you have one large distortion of the "free market."

You can create a better future for our country, and our

children, by counting all the costs of the project you are proposing, and comparing it to the true cost, including the subsidies and the harm done to our families and friends, of all alternatives. If you do this, you will help your audience make better choices.

Overcome Those Who Deny the Need for Change

When you accept the challenge to provide leadership, you can expect some pushback. It may comfort you to know you will be joining a long list of people who improved society over the objections of people who stood to profit if things did not change. History is full of attempts by citizens and authority figures to stifle the spread of new knowledge.

In 1632, Galileo wrote a book claiming that the universe revolved around the sun rather than the earth, which caused a stir. The official view was that the universe revolved around the earth. Galileo based his beliefs on close scientific observations through a new invention—the telescope. Because he had better scientific equipment, he was able to challenge the commonly held beliefs of the time.[1] Those who disagreed with him wanted Galileo's ideas taught as theory rather than fact-based science. This was something Galileo refused to do.[2]

In his late sixties he was sentenced to life in prison for teaching this controversial idea. Nine years after his sentence, Galileo

---

1   http://www-history.mcs.st-and.ac.uk/Biographies/Galileo.html
2   Galileo Galilei: Father of Modern Science by Rachel Hilliam 2005

died while still in custody.[1,2] **This was a heavy price to pay for trying to introduce scientific fact into public dialogue.**

Galileo was simply challenging a widely held belief by presenting new evidence. He was not issuing a warning. When it comes to warnings, the same set of defense mechanisms comes into play but with more casualties.

Take the sinking of the ship Titanic. The captain ignored a daylong series of warnings from other ships' captains who had sailed the route the day before and had narrowly escaped a collision. The captain had been warned that dangerous icebergs lay ahead,[3] yet the Titanic's lookouts were not placed on alert or issued binoculars.[4] Because leadership failed to listen to warnings, 1,490 people lost their lives.[5] These lives could have been spared by a simple course correction.

Closer to home we have Camp Lejeune, where warnings about polluted underground water supplies were ignored for years.[6] More than one million military personnel and their family members[7] were unnecessarily exposed to

1   http://www.chacha.com/question/how-long-was-galileo-imprisoned

2   http://www-history.mcs.st-and.ac.uk/Biographies/Galileo.html

3   http://www.ehow.com/info_85152_did-captain-titanic-ignore-warnings.html

4   http://www.titanicstory.com/interest.htm

5   http://www.titanicstory.com/interest.htm

6   http://www.stripes.com/news/camp-lejeune-water-contamination-timeline-1.100991

7   http://abcnews.go.com/US/sick-families-nc-military-base-water-contamination-finally/story?id=16670758

avoidable health risks because officials ignored warnings. According to the Veterans Administration, those exposed to this contaminated water now have higher than normal rates of cancers of the male breast, esophagus, lungs, bladder, and skin, as well as rare diseases of the liver, kidney and lymph glands.[1]

I could go on.

People comfortable in their beliefs will go to great lengths to reject new knowledge.

I lecture frequently on our future and the choices that we face. Over time, I have come to recognize a number of the standard defensive maneuvers.

The most popular defense is what I call "The Hypocrisy Probe." This is where the speaker is talking about threats to our environment and is challenged by his audience with questions like "Do you drive a Prius?" or "Do you eat organic?" If the speaker answers either of these questions with "no," he has been positioned to look like a hypocrite. The resistant student then feels justified in denying the validity of the new information being presented by the speaker. The best I have been able to do in this situation is to ask the questioner, "What does that have to do with the topic of this speech? I think you are trying to get the audience to take their attention away from the information I am presenting." After another try or two using additional techniques, many in the audience come to understand the motives of the questioner.

1   http://www.publichealth.va.gov/exposures/camp-lejeune/

Another defense is the "Do You Still Beat Your Wife?" scenario. In this case, an audience member trying to frustrate the delivery of a message asks the presenter, "Would you rather destroy the United States natural gas industry or continue to be dependent on Arab oil?" This question cannot be answered intelligently because important considerations such as energy conservation, wind power, solar power, geothermal, biofuels from algae, and a host of other wonderful, profitable alternatives have been left off the table.

I have found that the best rebuttal is to ask the questioners if their spouse still beats them. This usually gives them pause, long enough for me to say, "I will not ask you ridiculous questions if you will not ask them of me." And then I move on.

Then there is "The Junk Science Gambit." A non-scientist will stand up and point to piles of data and declare, "This is junk science." These individuals may have no knowledge of how the data was gathered or by whom.

The goal is not to understand—it is to create doubt in the mind of audience members.

This is then followed by a suggestion that no action be taken until we have "settled science," suggesting that there may be new knowledge around the corner. The cost of this delay is not trivial, however. Between the 1950s, when scientists first identified smoking as a contributing factor in disease, and the 1970s, when regulations were enacted,[1]

1   http://www.druglibrary.org/schaffer/library/studies/nc/nc2b.htm

16 million people died from smoking.[1] Many of these lives could have been saved, but the nation was lobbied by tobacco companies to wait for the science to "settle."

**Science by its very nature never "settles,"
and the people who advocate waiting
know that.**

As more and more people in our society have binoculars and are able to see the icebergs ahead, and as scientific knowledge explodes around us, the threats to public health and well-being will become more visible. You can help to ensure the future of your children by making sure that new information gets a fair hearing. This will require courage on your part and a support network willing to keep spreading the information.

---

[1]   http://www.yaleruddcenter.org/resources/upload/docs/what/industry/Foodtobacco.pdf

When You Don't Have *Power*, Use Your *Influence*

What is the difference between the meaning of *power* and the meaning of *influence?* How does that difference play out in improving society in ways you can be thankful for?

Remember how you felt when a uniformed officer of the law told you that you had done a bad thing? You were speeding, making too much noise and upsetting your neighbors, or stealing. Whatever it was, you knew in your rational mind that you'd better not do it again—or else.

Or else what?

Here is where the meaning of power comes in: if you don't shape up, you may be punished, whether you like it or not. Fines can be collected, jail time imposed, your rights to carry weapons or vote can be taken away—all because the policeman and the legal system have *power*. The will of society can legally be imposed on you.

Compare that to the meaning of *influence.* Influence is not imposed on you. You surrender to it voluntarily. When you go to church (voluntarily), and agree to accept certain conditions and constraints on your behavior (voluntarily), you are submitting to influence. If your church takes a position that you do not like, you can move to another congregation where the beliefs more comfortably align with your own. The same can be said when you consult your accountant, lawyer, or doctor. None of these professionals can make you do what they say. They can only make suggestions and spell out the consequences of non-compliance — but they do not have any power over your behavior.

If you don't like one doctor's advice, you can go to another.

As we look back at the tides of social change in our society, we frequently see power being used to enforce the status quo, and influence is frequently used to change it. Examples are everywhere in our history.

Legal slavery ended only after volunteers — responding to a higher moral authority — protested, lobbied, and formed underground railways. Their influence led to emancipation.

Early efforts by women to gain the right to vote resulted in the movement's leaders being whipped and imprisoned by those in power. Those in power were persuaded to change, but it took many decades.[1]

In the United States less than eighty years ago, children as young as eight years old labored fifteen-to-eighteen hours a day, seven days a week. Child labor ended, thanks to the struggle of many volunteers, but it took more than thirty years.[2]

The Civil Rights movement of the 1960s and 1970s was led by unknowns who gained influence as they repeated their message over and over. An influential leader spoke, and thousands of voluntary members of the movement followed.

Often the forces of *influence* clash with the forces of power. Those of you of a certain age can recall the awful videos

---

1   http://www.americaslibrary.gov/jb/jazz/jb_jazz_sufarrst_1.html

2   http://www.scholastic.com/teachers/article/history-child-labor

of Sheriff Bull Connor legally unleashing dogs on crowds of volunteers, who were marching peacefully with Dr. Martin Luther King Jr. in the effort to end legal segregation.

Even the Thanksgiving holiday itself reflects the effects of influence.

Sarah Hale, who was a magazine writer and activist, began a campaign in 1827 to have a unified national day of giving thanks.[1] She preached, wrote, organized, and recruited volunteer followers. Her efforts spanned thirty-one years and finally resulted in a declaration by President Lincoln. The president used his power to establish a national holiday, but he was responding to the influence of Sarah Hale and her followers.[2]

When you start your project, unless you are blessed to be in a role where you actually have power over all the pieces that need to change, you will need to use influence to persuade people to change. This means that you need to adopt a vocabulary rooted in values, morality, and emotion. The extent to which people will enlist in your cause will be equal to their perception that you are right. You will need to be able to articulate the full *cost* of the alternatives and frame your arguments with *values* in mind.

1   http://womenshistory.about.com/od/thanksgiving/a/sarah_hale_letter.htm

2   http://womenshistory.about.com/od/thanksgiving/a/hale_thanksday.htm

Measure Your Progress

I could truthfully tell you that 42 percent of high-school students had sex in 2013—and horrify you. Or I could tell you that the percentage of sexually active high-school students has dropped from 54 percent in 1991 to 42 percent in 2013—and make you feel that things are at least moving in the right direction.[1]

I could tell you that almost one in fourteen (7 percent) of all American youth between the ages of sixteen and twenty-four lack a high-school credential of any kind—and you would fear for our state and our country. Or I could tell you that twenty-five years ago 11 percent of American youth lacked any high-school credentials—and you would understand that our graduation rate is actually getting better.[2]

In both cases the second piece of data is vitally important in assessing society's health—without it, you don't know if things are getting better or worse. Yet it is common practice in public debate today to cite only one piece of data without context. As you launch your effort, you will be well served by documenting your starting point data.

You also need to make sure you are counting the right things—not the easy things.

---

1   Sexually Active Teens—Child Trends Data Bank http://www. childtrends.org/?indicators=sexually-active-teens

2   National Center for Educational Statistics, Status dropout rates 1990-2012 https://nces.ed.gov/fastfacts/display.asp?id=16

The examples are legion. For example, if more children got into scouting, more churches increased efforts to care for the poor, fewer women had unwanted pregnancies, more children got better reading scores, and fewer farmers contaminated the water supply with pesticides, GDP would not budge. But quality of life would improve.

Some communities have tons of data such as arrest records, false fire alarms, graduation rates, and so forth scattered throughout the files of many different agencies. This makes the task of assessing the well-being of the community difficult.

One community that does pool data from different agencies is Charlotte, North Carolina. In partnership with the city of Charlotte, Mecklenburg County, Foundation for the Carolinas, and roughly forty other nonprofits, United Way in 2013 began spearheading an effort to improve the way agencies collect data from students and the homeless. The idea is to identify the services they need when they first seek assistance. United Way now has provided each of the sixteen agencies in the project with aggregate data on how the children they serve were performing before the agencies began serving them. They use measures such as grades, attendance, and in-school and out-of-school suspensions. Trending data will be shared with all cooperating agencies to make sure that clients are receiving required help in a coordinated way and that factors leading to success can be identified for replication.

One additional challenge is that many record-keeping programs report only on failures: the number of violent

crimes, traffic accidents, deaths due to smoking, days of unhealthy air quality, and the like. These are called lagging indicators. They report on things that have already occurred,
over which we have no control.

Other indicators are more predictive. These are called
leading indicators. Examples include the percentage of children who enter the second grade knowing their alphabet
(predictive of future success in school),[1] the percentage of
pregnant women who are overweight (the children of overweight moms experience more health problems),[2,3,4] and the
percentage of teens who do not smoke (teens who smoke
experience higher disease rates later in life).[5,6] These leading
indicators are often not collected or, if they are collected,
they typically are not in the headlines.

Some communities have recognized the opportunity
to collect and trend both lagging and leading indicators
over time. These communities are able to identify emerging
problems—and applaud and support successful interven-
tions. The city of Jacksonville, Florida, has been a pioneer in
this area and is worth imitating. Since 1985, the Jacksonville
Community Council, Inc. (JCCI) has been developing a sys-

---

1   http://blogs.edweek.org/edweek/inside-school-research/2011/04/
     the_disquieting_side_effect_of.html

2   http://www.unsw.edu.au/)

3   http://www.webmd.com/baby/news/20090210/obesity-carries-preg-
     nancy-risks

4   http://www.nlm.nih.gov/medlineplus/news/fullstory_132170.html

5   http://mumsinscience.net/NEW/2012/02/smoking-negative-impact-
     developing-teen-brains/

6   http://www.livestrong.com/article/197602-the-health-risks-of-teen-
     age-smoking/

214 RESCUING YOUR LOCAL ECONOMY

tem to track indicators of the quality of life in Jacksonville
and surrounding communities.

JCCI publicly monitors and tracks fifty indicators—five
for each of ten target areas, including education, economy,
natural environment, social environment, arts and culture,
health, government, transportation, and public safety.

Each year a citizen-led review committee looks at all
fifty indicators, selects the "red flags" and "gold stars" for
Jacksonville, and develops a call-to-action. The organization puts together the annual progress report and hosts a
press release event.

The target areas and indicators maintained under each
can be found on www.communitysnapshot.org. They also
have the data collected and archived for the past thirty
years. They are able to answer questions for folks regarding
the historical data.

This link will show you what the current Quality of
Life Report looks like: http://issuu.com/jcci/docs/2014_
qol/1?e=3421855/11148930.

For example, in Jacksonville the public health records
revealed that births to teen moms, per 1,000 pregnant teens,
steadily dropped from a high of twenty-five in 1989 to a low
of ten several decades later.[1] The records also revealed that
the St. Johns River, which runs through the center of town,
is getting cleaner.

The report is updated annually; it often drives the agen-
da of local government and other groups. The Pew Partnership for Civic Change, the United Nations, and the International Community Indicators Consortium have highlighted

---

1   http://www.doh.state.fl.us/family/tpp/stats/stats.html

JCCI's work.[1]

An annual survey, donated by *American Public Dialogue*, provides additional information on the community's perception of the quality of life. Detailed reference data, including charts and graphs, are also provided for those who wish to explore these trends further. The document serves as a roadmap for community improvement, telling the community where they are, where they were, and the distance yet to be traveled.

As you start planning your project, make sure you reach out to others who may have already developed various useful metrics, or better yet, participate in a pooling of metrics that benefits both the contributors of the data and the policy makers who rely on it.

Springer Press has published a series of six "Best Cases" on various admirable community efforts from around the country that will be a good support for your effort. Additional tutoring and introduction to role models can be found at the Community Indicators Consortium at www.community-indicators.net.

---

1   http://rally-foundation.org/projects/neighborhood-info initiatives/
     resources/Community%20indicator%20Measurements/A%20com-
     munity%20Indicators%20Case%20Study.pdf/@@preview_prcvider

Look to Retirees
and Millennials for Talent

RETIREES: A funny thing happened back in the late 1940s—lots of young women got pregnant at the same time. Some point to more than 13 million[1] servicemen coming home to their lonely girlfriends. Guess what happened over the next few years?

Births went from 2.5 million in 1940 to 3.5 million in 1950.

As little brothers and sisters were born, annual births hit 4 million in 1954 and stayed above 4 million until 1965 when births finally dropped back to 3.7 million. Thus were created the "Boomers."

Fast-forward to today. As they approach their mid-sixties, those born in the 1950s are now stepping away from full-time paid employment, presenting a major opportunity for change agents.

The Boomers age group is quite unlike previous generations.

Because of better health care and the existence of Medicare, the average 50-year-old today will live six years longer than they would have in 1950.[2] And they are much better educated.

---

1   http://wiki.answers.com/Q/How_many_Americans_fought_in_
     World_War_2

2   http://www.prb.org/pdf11/TodaysResearchAging22.pdf

In 1950 only one in four of all U.S. citizens over twenty-five had a high school diploma, and only one in twenty had a college degree.[1] Today, more than sixty-three years later, over half of those over twenty-five have a high school diploma, and one in three has at least one college degree.[2] Many of these will continue their education through their career. What an outstanding success story for our country!

Among those hitting sixty-five this year, around one in ten have a master's, professional, or doctorate degree. Another one in ten have a college degree; one in four have some college and one third have a high school diploma.[3] This trend will continue, because their younger brothers and sisters are even more educated and experienced.

If you graduate from high school, you are likely to live seven years longer than someone who doesn't, and if you earn college degree you are likely to live an additional two years beyond high school graduates.[4,5] These individuals who are well educated and no longer employed will be around for quite a while.

Recruiting these retirees to your team will be beneficial to you—and to them. Although they may not be paid dollars for their time, they will be receiving emotional compensation.

1   http://www.census.gov/hhes/socdemo/education/data/cps/historical/fig2.jpg

2   ibid.

3   http://www.census.gov/hhes/socdemo/education/data/cps/2012/tables.html

4   http://www.cbc.ca/news/health/story/2008/03/12/education-life-expectancy.html

5   http://abclocal.go.com/kabc/story?section=news/health&;id=8664380

Loneliness is a health hazard. People with active social connections add even more years to their lives. One study compared the death rates of older altruistic volunteers to those of similar age who do not volunteer and found that the volunteers lived appreciably longer lives, over and above the gains realized from higher education.[1]

Every single day since 2010 we've had somewhere around 10,000 of these well-educated Boomers hit their sixty-fifth birthday and approach a new stage of life.[2] These people are an incredible resource—retirement no longer equals old age.

At the same time we have a host of social problems. In 2009, 41 percent of all babies born in the United States were born to unwed mothers,[3] resulting in a large percentage of children with no male role models. Nearly 40 percent of all fourth graders in this country cannot read at grade level, and this number rises to 60 percent for children coming from poor families.[4] I could go on and on with these types of statistics. Our communities are crying out for seasoned leadership in efforts ranging from public safety to environmental protection.

Contributing to solving these and many other problems can be a source of joy, inspiration and longer life for our newly arriving seasoned reinforcements.

Back in the 1940s, talented mature leaders were recruit-

1   http://www.livescience.com/15978-volunteers-live-longer.html
2   http://tucsoncitizen.com/medicare/2012/03/16/turning-65-enrolling-in-medicare/
3   http://www.cdc.gov/nchs/fastats/unmarry.htm
4   http://www.amazon.com/Why-Kids-Cant-Read-Challenging/dp/1578863821

ed to the war effort. They accepted one dollar a year in salary while holding very high positions in the White House and elsewhere. Their children can now do the same thing if room is made for them and leadership will think big enough.

As the credentials of the volunteer pool have improved, organizations that use volunteers may need to rethink the assignments they offer. I keep hearing of highly trained people seeking to align with a substantial organization that could use their training and talent, only to be asked to be greeters or drivers.

Some who study this field believe that paid leaders in nonprofits and local government organization are hesitant to bring in highly trained older volunteers because they perceive the volunteers as a threat to their own status. If you have not yet begun such recruiting, this may be a useful internal dialog to have.

A number of national resources exist to help both retirees and local efforts through this transition. The Senior Corps has a large library of resources on how to recruit, retain, and maximize the contribution of our newly arrived talent pool. You can find them at www.Nationalservice.gov. Civic Ventures, www.civicventures.org, has books and other materials to help both local governments and other organizations create meaningful roles for retirees. Another good resource is a book called *The Encore Careers Handbook* by Marci Alboher.

You can help by recommending recruitment of this trained labor pool that is currently underutilized and bored. Organizations and causes that can and will fully use their talent will benefit immensely.

MILLENIALS: A second major pool of talent currently underutilized is our twenty-somethings and early thirty-year-olds. If you analyze the demographics of all elected officials at the city, county, state, and federal levels in the United States, only 5 percent, or one in twenty, are younger than thirty-five years old.[1]

This age disparity has significant implications because down the road these younger involved citizens will go on to make up the core of our national leadership. More than half of the members of Congress, governors, and presidents of the United States were first elected to office when they were between eighteen and thirty-five years old.[2] In electoral politics we are not on that mentoring path.

The National Association of Counties conducted a study that focused on this disparity at the county level. Elected officials were asked if our current system encourages the best people to run for offices, discourages them from running, or if the system makes no difference.[3] The majority, 66 percent, said that the current system discourages the best people from running for office. Only 9 percent said our system encourages our best leaders to run for office.[4]

1   http://www.yeonetwork.org/content/about-young-electeds

2   http://www.eagleton.rutgers.edu/research/documents/YELPFullReport.pdf

3   http://www.eagleton.rutgers.edu/research/documents/YELPFullReport.pdf

4   http://www.naco.org/research/pubs/Documents/County%20Management%20and%20Structure/Research%20County%20Management%20and%20Structure/2012%20National%20Survey%20of%20County%20Elected%20Officials%20Opinions%20from%20the%20

Fortunately, some good role models exist that we can imitate to bring about change in this area.

The mayor of Fort Worth, Texas, decided she wanted to take steps to grow what she called the "next generation of leaders."[1]

She sent a message out through churches, civic organizations, and schools, asking them to spread the word that she was looking for future civic leaders between the ages of twenty-one and forty that she could work with. The only real requirement was that they have an interest in, and concern for, the larger society. Over a few months roughly 300 names were gathered. Leadership Fort Worth facilitated the process. A list of the features of an attractive community was posted on social media so that the young professionals could discuss them, vote on them, and otherwise refine the dimensions they felt would create an attractive place to live. Using social media the young professionals narrowed the list to five focus areas: public transit, employment opportunities, urban development, education, and community leadership development. After the online rank ordering and discussion period, everyone was invited to a day-long event called the Big Brainstorm where the members of the group had an opportunity to meet and develop specific focus areas with high leverage potential within each of the big four topic areas.

At the conclusion of the event, the members were asked to select one of the four focus areas. Of the original 300 potential future leaders who had been identified, 120 agreed

Front%20Lines%20of%20Local%20Government.pdf

1   http://www.youtube.com/watch?v=2RqqkYeTymY

to serve on eight-month task forces to impact the problem that captured their attention. The other 180 agreed to be a resource and help when asked. The task-force process was managed by Leadership Fort Worth in conjunction with the mayor's office. All four groups were required to reach actionable conclusions that would be reported back to the community in September. The reports were dynamic and impactful, including a pilot program on more nutritional school lunches, the securing of grant and local funding for a bike-share program, an online employment resource site, and a partnership with Better Block to assist local urban villages. (Better Block is a nonprofit promoting the growth of healthy and vibrant neighborhoods.)

One year later, approximately half of the original 120 are still active in the task forces, and many of the other participants drop in to help when called on. While the task forces worked, the mayor's office hosted monthly brown bag lunches where top level civic leaders, like school superintendents, law enforcement officials, and transportation system administrators engaged in frank discussion and were available for open question and answer sessions. A series of "happy hours with a purpose" continued to be held around town, where the young leaders could meet and get acquainted with their senior counterparts. They bowled with city council, got a behind the scenes look at the Dallas / Ft. Worth airport, and became much more familiar with the city that needs them to lead it into the future.

We do not have to act like the future is a bus coming toward us as we stand still and watch. We can take the driver's seat and steer toward the world we want to see. You can help by thinking of young potential future leaders and introducing them to the process of leadership and civic responsibility.

As a leader yourself, you know how you have been mentored and have guided those who are following you. These experiences benefited both you and your colleagues. You can harvest all of this, and can make an enormous contribution.

Conclusion

The need for change is obvious, as are the challenges to bringing it about. Your role will require you to carefully define the kinds of activities that bring you joy, the issues that energize you, and your own strengths and weakness. Once you have done that, you do not have to reinvent the wheel. You can start from the back of this book first—recruit talent, define the problem you and they want to solve, and begin to look for success stories you can imitate. Carefully craft your goal statement and metrics, and use a vocabulary of emotion, morality and family.

Be patient with yourself. Much of the change talked about in this book—from smoking cessation to race relations, to women's rights, to child-abuse prevention, to literacy—required decades of dedicated work by heroic people.

They made society better. And so can you.

Let us begin.

Afterword

As you have been reading this book, you have learned about many inspirational success stories. These and many more are stored for public use and imitation at www.The-OptimisticFuturist.org. I would like to see this inspirational collection expand by adding contributions from you.

If you pull off a replicable success (even a duplicate of one of those presented here), please write it up and send it to us so we can add it to the collection. If you look at the top bar of the website, you will see "Your Success Stories" for guidelines.

And of equal importance, if you know of other replicable success stories that can guide other leaders, please let us know so we may reach out for permission to add them to the collection as well.

About the Author

Francis Koster received his doctorate from the Program for the Study of the Future at the University of Massachusetts in 1982, where he studied the public policy implications of likely national and global futures and their impact on the United States. He focuses his attention on issues concerning the basic life support systems of air, water, food, energy, environment, and the public health consequences of how society meets its needs in these areas.

Of particular fascination to him is trying to answer the question, "Why don't leaders listen to warnings?" In his view, just telling the captain of the *Titanic* that there is an iceberg ahead has a low chance of causing evasive action. His studies convinced him that you also have to say, "If you turn right 15 degrees, you will be safe." When you add the solution to the warning, decision-makers are more likely to take corrective action. Without a solution, the warning is suppressed.

Following service in the National Guard and the Peace Corps, Koster began his career as a higher-education reformer in the '60s and '70s. His focus shifted to energy policy during the oil embargoes of the '70s, during which time he set up and ran the University of Massachusetts'

Toward Tomorrow Fair; the university's Alternative Energy Program; the Tennessee Valley Authority's Renewable Energy program; and consulted with many of the nation's major utilities on energy conservation and renewable energy programs. In this same era, working with the U.S. Department of Energy, he developed and ran the first assessment of how counties can attain energy self-sufficiency. President Ronald Reagan cited his Franklin County study as a national model.

Recruited to a rapidly expanding health-care organization in the 1990s, Koster established himself as a pioneer in the application of information technologies in health care. His efforts demonstratively improved health care through ubiquitous deployment of electronic medical records, thereby making patient information available over the internet, including "Telehealth," among many other initiatives. In 2008 he retired from the position of Vice President for Innovation for The Nemours Foundation—one of the largest children's health systems in the United States, which now has more than 650 full-time physicians, two regional children's hospitals, and more than twenty pediatric clinics.

Since 2008, Koster has provided services to the University of North Carolina Nutrition Research Institute, the Duke University Graduate School of Nursing, the Duke University Center for Health Informatics, the Catawba College Center for the Environment, and other clients.

In addition to his consulting practice, Koster writes newspaper columns explaining problems facing America, and introduces the reader to replicable and proven solutions already in place somewhere in the United States. These columns, along with a collection of similar stories prepared by others, can be found at www.TheOptimisticFuturist.org.

Dr. Koster is married to Dr. Carol Spalding, president of Rowan-Cabarrus Community College in North Carolina. Like other parents and grandparents their age, they worry over, and cheer for, four adult children and three grandchildren.

In addition to this book, he is the author of *Rescuing School Kids: America's Success Stories* and *Discovering the New America: Where Local Communities Are Solving National Problems.*

CPSIA information can be obtained at www.ICGtesting.com
Printed in the USA
LVOW11s0001230816

501376LV00001B/143/P